PERSONALITY TYPES

The Psychology of the Enneagram

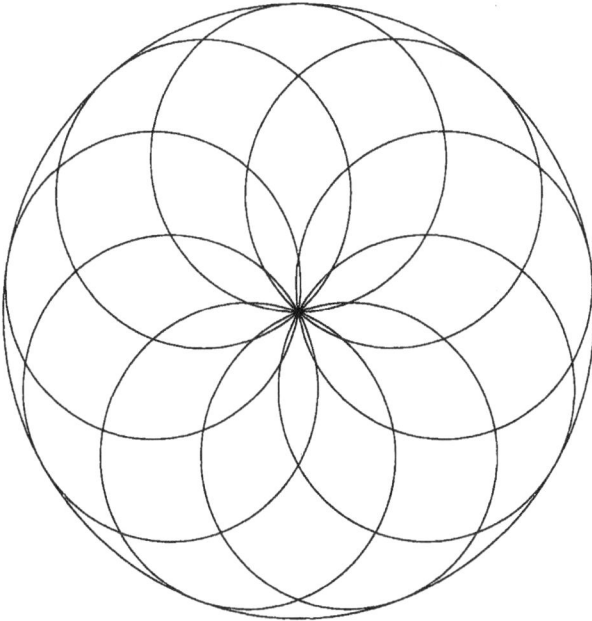

Revised Edition

Richard Leggett

NEPTUNE PUBLISHING

First published 2005
Revised 2024
Published by Neptune Publishing

© Richard Leggett
email: rleggett7@gmail.com

ISBN 978-1-0369-0039-7

Cover design by Katie Deith

Acknowledgment

I would like to acknowledge the assistance of Felicity Bradley and Brian Snellgrove, for their unstinting efforts to check my technical findings; and of Rosemary Steel, for providing some remarkable psychiatric case study material. Without them, this book would not have been written.

The accuracy of the technical findings has been established to be 95% or better. Any proposed amendments, as well as comments and suggestions of any kind, will be gratefully received.

| Enneagram | | Outsider | |
type	orientation	state	Observations
One	towards	separated	abandoned and lost: need to be guided
Two	towards	negated	unwanted: emotional abandonment
Three	against	denied	humiliated, rejected: need to prove worth
Four	away from	estranged	banished into life, as if from a higher estate
Five	away from	disempow-ered	need to regain rational control of the self and its space
Six	towards	separated	abandoned: need for something to adhere to
Seven	against	negated	excluded from living: missing out
Eight	against	denied	without means; held back
Nine	away from	estranged	need for something to identify with

Orientation is defined in tabulation No.2 of appendix No.1. The outsider state is treated under its own heading in each of chapters three to eleven.

Contents

Chapter 1

INTRODUCTION

Background

This book is an experimental presentation of the Enneagram as a uniquely informative and enlightening psychological aid to daily living, which may be used on a practical basis by anyone in almost any circumstance.

The origins of the Enneagram, as a form of Eastern wisdom traditionally imparted by a teacher for the spiritual advancement of the student, are treated elsewhere in the literature.

Application

From the standpoint of the Enneagram, personality may be likened to a jigsaw puzzle. A slight knowledge of a person enables a small number of the pieces, with some guesswork, to be put tentatively in place, but most of the puzzle remains a blank space. A more detailed knowledge of him, worked into an understanding of the Enneagram and of his Enneagram type, results in clusters of pieces being added. The greater the knowledge of the person, and understanding of his type over the spectrum of its categories and by affinity of traits, the more this is so.

The reader who can establish his Enneagram type (and subtype) should be in a position to know the rationale of his being in life: what it is that he has to learn and to give out; why he views life and himself as he does, whether this be positively or negatively, and with how much realism and morality; the modalities and strength of his connection with life (which in the Four or the Five can be oblique or fragile; and in the Five, elementary); why he is drawn to what he is by way of interests, the deciding factor being not the interests per se but how he perceives and goes about them; whether he has disharmony or tension within himself or in interaction, and the cause (the types to generate tension are typically the One, Five, and Six); what makes him happy or sad, and why, in so far as he attaches importance to emotional wellbeing; why he succeeds – or fails – in relationships; and what features he has, as a composite being, that are healthy or unhealthy, strong or weak – remembering that 'strong' may not equate with 'healthy', and recognizing that those features which are unhealthy merit his attention.

Parents having knowledge and understanding of the Enneagram types of themselves and the family would have a head start in forestalling or resolving disagreement, and in reducing the chances of their offspring going down a wrong track in life.

First steps

The Enneagram is a representation of human nature in all its states and orientations, and is generally depicted as nine points at the circumference of a circle, the points being variously linked. In my own design, the links as simple lines are dispensed with. Subject to exceptions (see chapter two), each person has one of the nine points as his personality type. This type describes his nature in outline.

Again subject to exceptions, he also has a subtype (termed a 'wing' in the traditional teachings), which is one or other of the points adjoining that of the type. As a unit, type and subtype describe his nature with more precision.

Thus, someone who has the One for his type has either the Nine or the Two for his subtype; someone who has the Nine for his type has either the Eight or the One for his subtype; and so on. Whatever the level of psychological health, the points which comprise the type and subtype do not alter.

Authors have given the types an assortment of names (see 'Comment on name of type' in chapters three to eleven). In the text, a type is referred to in words (e.g. 'the One'), and a type with its subtype in numbers (e.g. 1-9, or 'One with Nine').

Whether new to the Enneagram or not, the reader is urged to be cautious in the assessment of type, and not to imagine that a dependable judgment can be made either from a general impression, or where needed facts are missing. In this respect, it is to be regretted that in the literature examples of type are wrong as often as they are right (see 'Assessment elaborated' in chapter two). Traits have even been thoughtlessly assigned to types which they patently do not possess.

Each type has many resemblances to one, or two, others. Someone, for instance, who supposes himself to be a Two or a Three would do well to review the Seven; or supposing himself to be a Four, to review the Two. Resemblances do not stop at resonances within the Enneagram: many Sixes will have been misled into believing that they are Eights (see next chapter); and a social and attentive Nine can look very much like a Two – or a social and easygoing Nine, very much like a Seven.

It is asserted by some authors that it is for the reader to determine his type, since he knows himself best. This is a questionable statement. Habit patterns of thought and action do indeed constitute evidence of type (but which type, and why?); so do traits that are not noted because value is not attributed to them, and ones that are disowned ("That's not me!").

The notion that type can be assessed from a sense of 'feel' in observing body language, way of talking etc. is false, ignoring as it does the gamut of psychological defence and disguise. As to the usefulness of self-assessment in a group setting, it is pertinent to remind the reader who might be drawn to this that recognition of type by comparison or contrast, and conformity of view, can be induced or acted out in a social setting.

Assessment of type

In order to be of use in assessment, a trait must be established to relate with some degree of certainty to one or two types, and preferably to one only. No deduction can be made from traits which could be those of anyone, e.g. kind, active. As a rule, to determine the motivation is to have identified the type.

Each of the nine chapters on the types provides a grounding in traits that are amenable to assessment, and can be supplemented by the corresponding profiles in appendix No.4. The uneven spread of examples in the appendix is inevitable, some (e.g. the Five or the Seven) being rated by the world at large as higher achievers than others (e.g. the Four or the Nine). In the main, examples are confined to the famous – or infamous – so that should the reader wish to research them for himself, he will have ample material in the public domain from which to do so.

To illustrate by reference to some traits which have more than one possible correlation, the Three is set on standing out by winning, as if in a race, and thereby affirms his worth. The Six keeps up to par with his peers – perhaps he betters them – and is respected and acknowledged to belong with them; or he may have a reason of his own to be seen to do well, e.g. in being thought to be less capable. With his enthusiasm and desire to be where the action is, competitive success may come easily to the Seven. Any one of these could be a natural winner, only the motivation distinguishing them. The Three may say to himself, "I can outdo my opponent", his focus being on himself; the Six, "I battle to win against my opponent", on to whom he brings his focus; and the Seven, "I am confident of being enabled to win."

In the Three, the effect of the projection of image is pleasing and persuasive, and in furtherance of his goals. In the Seven, its projection ensures that his attitudes and responses tally with what they are expected to be, and that social discomfort is avoided. It is the Seven – not the Two – who has a repertoire of selves from which he can choose the version which will be suited to the occasion, whether to gain attention, concession, or advantage; to feel safe (7-6); or as a game of excitement or fantasy.

The image of the social climber who is intent on securing a respected status within the institutional mainstream is that of the Six. In his motivation to succeed, he could be mistaken for a Three; and in a post of personal assistant, for a Two.

Types for whom the projection of image is a worthless concept are the One, Four, Nine, and with slight reservation the Five.

In feeling unwanted, the Two is lonely and hurt, and at the extreme emotionally desperate. To feel abandoned or not part of a group is, for the Six, to be looked down on as not deserving, and to be taken notice of grudgingly or not at all. To be excluded is, for the Seven, to be missing out; if this is perceived by him as tantamount to being 'on the wrong wavelength', an adjustment of image can be made. Any one of these could experience envy.

To have a craving to be liked, within a framework of social acceptance, is a trait of the Six (6-7).

As a compliant youngster, the One respects and obeys authority figures, that being the right thing for him to do. The Two derives emotional contentment and a feeling of belonging from meeting others' needs and wants, and from having his own met in response. For the Six, to obey is to be secure: to be on the 'right side' of authority. To the Seven, doing what he is told promises greater freedom of movement:

lines of communication that are open and harmonious mean that requests are granted that might otherwise be met with refusal. To ingratiate oneself, in the sense of "Let's do something to keep him sweet", or to repair damage that the behaviour has caused, is a device of the Two or the Seven; what for the Six is the 'right side' has now become the 'good side'. The 'doormat' as a person is most likely 2-3 or 5-6.

To rebel is a behavioural pattern of the Six or the Seven (7-6). Boundaries may be tested out ("Can I get away with this without being told off or punished?"), by the Six to establish where the limits are, and by the Seven for latitude; or reassurance sought ("If I behave badly, will I still be loved and wanted?"). The hardened rebel as a Six acts in conformity with image, validating the low expectations that others have of him ("They make no secret of what they think of me, so what's the use of trying to play by their rules?"). The Seven insists on getting something out of life, and if orthodox and legitimate routes seem closed to him, as a rebel he is not slow in discovering ones that are neither of these – and exciting. In rebel mode, either of them can be a fatalist.

Indecisiveness is caused in the One by the prospect of his actions making a bad situation worse, for which he sees himself being blamed – and would blame himself. In the Six, a major cause is a conflict of impulses (see chapter eight); others are apprehension that a decision will have a chain reaction, throwing all into disarray and necessitating its reappraisal, or confusion over which authority he should be guided by. The passive Nine from whom a decision is awaited in vain has to be told what to do, or to have it done for him. As with the indecisiveness into which for the Six it shades, procrastination stems from security considerations, as for the employee who waits for months before having a show-down with his boss over an injustice, fancying that his career will be harmed, or that he will encounter hostility from colleagues – his peers – for souring the working atmosphere.

If his enthusiasm is quick to expend itself, the Seven can be sidetracked from finishing one task into embarking on another, not resuming the first until or unless obliged to. Wasting time toying with what is of no consequence, instead of tackling the one job that must be done, is an automatic mechanism of resistance by the Nine, who is also the person who makes a rushed and useless effort at the last moment.

The autocrat is a self-righteous One for whom there is but one way, other ways being temptations to be resisted; the self-important and controlling Three (3-4); the arrogant Five who regards the evaluation of views not his own as a waste of time and energy; the Six who has ones that are strongly held and contested – psychologically, they may be strongly held because contested –, or who feels insecure if shown to be indecisive; or the Eight for whom debate is a slowing of pace, and consensus therefrom a weakening of effect.

In the role of the persuasive salesman and speaker, the Three makes his audience feel empowered by its possession of the ideas that he puts forward ("I have what you need"). The persuasive Six (6-7), or the Seven with a heavy Six subtype, rouses his audience to join forces with him, in feeling as he does, in the cause that he represents: he needs them on his side.

Aggression is rooted in competitiveness (the Three); the desire to secure his position against threat or opposition (the Six); insistence, the object of his aggression being an obstacle to be removed (the Seven); or strength of means (the Eight).

Harking back to school days, a harsh regime is associated with the One; but that is only half the story. Many of the teachers whose fearsome reputation preceded them were not Ones but Fives, who used those teaching methods which they believed promote the value of learning, inculcating obedience to rules, industriousness, moderation of behaviour, and quiet. To the One, control is the safeguard of order; to the Five, control acclimatizes the student to the ethos of a thorough education.

Nostalgia for a state of happiness that can never be recovered, and which hovers in the imagination between the real and the idealized as a sense of separation, is a sentiment of the Four. The nostalgic Nine lives in his mind in the past that he knew, and is out of sympathy with the change that has wrought the present.

Appearances may have to be searched for the substance behind them. Here is a hypothetical example of what could ensue from the behaviour of a man who is a Six, and who does not know his own mind. The man shares a passionate kiss with a woman with whom he is acquainted, and to which he is responsive despite having a partner. On the social grapevine she broadcasts the news; he maintains, however, that she assaulted him. He has betrayed his partner: in terms of his type, he has jeopardized his emotional security source. He feels demeaned before his friends and neighbours: again in terms of his type, his sense of social self-respect has been dented. Angry at himself, he disowns the sentiment by projecting it on to the woman – the Six being the type to engage in psychological projection.

When suspicions without grounds are entertained about a partner's infidelity, the prudent Six as the other partner should check that those suspicions are not a projection of what he or she – the Six – has in mind to do.

At the height of the stockmarket boom in internet technology in 1999, a stock analyst who was one of the star performers in the U.S., with a regular spot on television, and whom company executives were clamouring to meet, was privately disparaging stocks which he was recommending investors to buy; he is a Three. In an internal email he described one of the stocks on his 'buy' list as "a piece of shit." Yet his employers would have rated him as outstandingly committed (i.e. as a Six), given the scale of business that he generated for them. In fact, he was motivated by the exponential rise of his income – and nothing more. When big money is at stake, the claims and track record of a Three should not be taken on trust, but examined for the fabrication and inconsistencies which in a dishonest Three will be there for the uncovering.

Integration and disintegration

Mention has been made of the lines which connect the points of the Enneagram as depicted to each other. These are the lines of integration and disintegration, paths which function as accentuators of growth (integration) or of regression (disintegration), subsidiary to the expression of the type and subtype. The feature is unusual but not rare, and may or may not be permanent once begun; someone who is psychologically unhealthy could disintegrate for a period of months or years, in due course leaving the line, having been restored in health. The combinations are interpreted in appendix No.2.

My understanding is that the subtype does not of itself integrate or disintegrate.

Chapter 2

GUIDELINES

Source material

The student of the Enneagram should start by observing those with whom he is most familiar – himself included –, since they are those about whom the largest amount of detail can be gathered with which to form an assessment.

Other good sources of material are newspapers, biographies, radio and television profiles, specialized directories, and encyclopaedias.

A wealth of information may be gleaned from obituaries. An example is Martin Wright, who died in 2001. Endowed with a technical (the Five) and aesthetic (the Four) cast of mind, he invented "simple and elegant medical instruments", "compact pieces of precision engineering that have become design classics in and beyond the medical world." During the Second World War he worked overseas as a pathologist – a profession of the Five –, his technical inventiveness developing from a lack of equipment: self-sufficiency is a trait of the Five not only in its autonomy, but also in the minimalist pragmatism of having to make do with a scarcity of resources. After the war he was recruited to a new unit of the Medical Research Council in Wales, which established for the study of lung disease in miners. His most influential instrument was the peak flow meter, used to diagnose respiratory diseases such as asthma and bronchitis; since its commercial production began, seven million have been sold. In 1957 he moved to the National Institute for Medical Research, where in studying breath alcohol he invented the roadside accident instrument, the breathalyzer. He is a Five, with the Four as subtype, i.e. 5-4.

Assessment elaborated

In the previous chapter, the reader was advised to be cautious in reaching conclusions as to type. Among those that are constantly misidentified are Sixes who are taken to be Eights, Fives taken to be various other types, Sevens taken to be Twos or Threes, various types taken to be Ones or Fours, and Sevens taken to be Eights.

The misidentifying of Sixes as Eights owes itself to a misconception that has been adopted throughout Enneagram literature; namely, that force of manner equates with the Eight, whereas what does is strength of means. The Six's weapon of habit is a combative or threatening posture; he is unsure how much force his opponent may have, or be disposed to avail himself of. The posture is a partial transfer of his insecurity on to the other person, who he hopes will either give in, or feel pressured into declaring himself, releasing the Six from the fear of not knowing what he is up against. If the Six is agitated, the threatening effect is increased; this is so irrespective of whether the state is genuine or put on as an act.

Hitler (a Six) would work himself up into a rage in order to browbeat a foreign emissary into caving in to his latest demand- but his emotions were expressed not because they were felt but for the effect that they had. By doing this he cowed his visitor, and boosted his own confidence.

Even a complex or obscure trait can be assigned to a type if its motivation, or the subtraits of which it is composed, can be discerned. The courage of the hero is a trait of the Six; but what of the brand of courage that is reckless? An example would be the passenger on a train who sees a person threatening to, or about to, do harm to another. As if momentarily taking leave of his rational self, drawing on reserves which he did not know that he had, and feeling no fear, on impulse he jumps up from his seat and, surprising himself and the other passengers, insists – or sees and hears himself insisting that the aggressor back off – which he does. This kind of hero is a Seven (7-6); the subtraits are trust in life, insistence, impulsiveness, and speed of movement. If the scenario is altered to one in which the heroic act is in the line of duty, that would replace trust in life as a subtrait, and the correlation would typically be with the Six (6-7); likewise if hero and victim were related or friends.

The host who makes a scene in the restaurant in front of his guests when the meal arrives and is not as it ought to be may be a Five who has been shown up, and is disempowered in having to rely on staff who are not answerable to him to put matters right. Other types who could react adversely are a bossy Two (2-3), an overbearing Three – who might also be minded to humiliate the staff by what he has to say –, an argumentative Six, or a loud-mouthed Seven who does not know when to stop.

To collect mementos is a tendency of the Five or the Nine. For the Five, a memento is an affirmation of the reality of his existence, and an agency through which by its asso-ciations the past can be revisited in memory. For the Nine, what is of the past as lived is comfortingly preserved in the memento. The trophy, less to reward a win than as a lucky find or catch, is a Five item.

Having determined what may be the type and subtype (but see 'Absence of subtype'), their relative strengths should be estimated, the type being heavier than the subtype. A heavy subtype can be mistaken for the type, whereas a light one may not be apparent. In case of doubt as to which is type and which subtype, attitudes in the formative years – if not in adulthood – resonate with the symbolism of the outsider state of the type. As a standard, in this book 'light' denotes a subtype of 15% of the total Enneagram content or less; 'medium', 16-34%; and 'heavy', 35% or more. To demonstrate with examples from appendix No.4, Thomas Jefferson and Charles Dickens are both 5-6. Dickens' subtype of about 40% is three times the strength of Jefferson's, which is why so many of his readers – and, in his recitations of later years, his audience – were moved (the pathos of the Six) by his tales of social misery. As a thinker, Jefferson formulated his ideas by observation – as did Dickens – but without a personal reaction. George Washington and Desmond Tutu are both 1-2. Tutu's warmth and displays of feeling (the Two) are legendary: his subtype is heavy; Washington's is medium. James Dean is 6-7, yet in school days he had the enthusiastic outlook of a Seven; the subtype is heavy.

When one or two traits are at variance with the rest, their correlation may be with another typology (e.g. the astrological birth chart), unless the feature is explained by admixture.

Admixture
Aptitudes or leanings which are absent from the nature of the type or subtype can indicate an admixture from a third type.

An admixture that is medium or heavy should be evident in assessment. 'Medium' would seem to denote about 15-20% of the total Enneagram content, and 'heavy' about 25-30%. Smaller ones are not so unusual, nor are they material to interpretation. The Five and the Seven are the types that predominate in this capacity, which could be due to the large range of functions that each has. A factor not to be confused by, in psychic diagnosis (see heading below), is that if subtype and admixture are heavy enough, the type can amount not to more than half of the total content, but to nearer 40%.

It is possible for an admixture to exceed the subtype in strength, and for its point to be adjacent to that of the type or subtype. Vincent van Gogh (see appendix No.4: the Four) has an admixture of the Five of about 25% of the total content, and a Three subtype of about 5%. Despite the proportions, he is 4-3 and not 4-5.

Thomas More (see next chapter) is a One with a heavy (30%) admixture of the Five. As a classicist and free thinker, he would be taken for a Five. He was, however, martyred upholding the authority decreed by his conscience (the One), not in defence of freedom of speech and the dissemination of knowledge (the Five). The reader will be able to find out for himself, in the course of chapter three, why the One is not- and would have no desire to be – a free thinker, without input from the Five.

Of the other examples in appendix No.4, in his screen role as the tramp, Charlie Chaplin (a Six) tempers pity (the Six) for his character with the genial humour of the Nine admixture. John Lennon (a Six) would not have had his streak of idealism without an admixture of the Five. The hunger for recognized achievement of Madonna (a Three) would not have been facilitated, as it so effectively was, by a provocative edge without an admixture of the Six.

Feats such as walking a tightrope or clearing a gorge on a motorcycle can correlate with the Five with an admixture of the Seven, or conversely the Seven with an admixture of the Five. Traits include skill of technique (the Five), and freedom of movement and trust in life (the Seven).

Absence of subtype

This feature is found most in the Three and the Seven. I have observed it occasionally in the Five, rarely in the Six and the Eight, and as yet not at all in the remaining four types.

A broad interpretation of the Seven with no subtype can be attempted from the examples to hand. He is his own person – he 'does his own thing' – in an area that to him is neither competitive nor contentious, nor one of fighting for a cause, impassioned sentiment, or protest. Antagonism is put up with, not reacted against, as it would be for 7-6 (or a Six).

Looser in his adherence to the interactive and comparative norms of belonging and regard, the Seven with no subtype is subject to less modification of manner than 7-6; his agenda is dictated by himself. In terms of the analogy in chapter nine of the route travelled, he is not bothered by whether he can pass other vehicles or is passed by them.

In stereotype the Seven as entertainer has a Six subtype, his art being a two-way process: to sense, and adapt himself to, what the audience will accept is a trait of the Six. If the entertainer is attentive to his audience, in delivering what pleases them, they in turn are attentive to him; they want his performance, and he their approbation. Marlene Dietrich (see appendix No.4: the Seven) counters this theory, in having no subtype. Her performance was delivered on her own terms; and the enigmatic image that she adopted, her own conception. Her audience responded to her – but how much did she respond to them?

Leni Riefenstahl directed *Triumph of the Will*, the documentary film of the National Socialist party congress of 1934 in Nuremberg.

The film is a masterpiece of innovative cinematic technique. For her part, she is forever tainted by her association with Hitler, who commissioned her to make the film at the shortest notice, by her account after much persistence. As a Seven with no subtype, she can be accused in hindsight of a self-absorbed naivety- as can many Sevens, and of thereby having a scant awareness of what was going on in the outside world – but not of being an accomplice in state propaganda to Joseph Goebbels, who resented her independence (the Seven as a free agent, which in filming she was), and with whom her relations were consequently fraught. Her aim would have been to make a record of the rally as a dynamic pageant and visual delight. In the 1920s she was a dancer, actress, and mountaineer. In recent decades she was a photographer of the Nuba tribe in Sudan, and of underwater marine life, having taken up deep-sea diving at the age of 72. She died in 2003, aged 101.

Nikolai Ezhov, in the 1930s the second most powerful man in the Soviet Union as People's Commissar for Internal Affairs, is of a category which in its excesses could be taken for an Eight, but he is in fact a Seven with no subtype. Such a person has been granted a completely free hand and is out of control; he has not acquired his standing by his own strength, hence the absence of an Eight component. A topical example is Kim Jong Il, ruler of North Korea.

With his opposition to the apartheid regime, Nelson Mandela could not have been a Seven with no subtype; he is 7-6, the subtype being heavy (see appendix No.4).

Defensiveness relates to the Six. Had Frank Sinatra been a Seven with no subtype and not 7-6 (see appendix No.4), he would not have retaliated as he did against those whom he felt slighted him.

In a country which is an Eight, liberalization corresponds to the Seven as subtype, and consolidation to the Nine. One wonders what will be the path of China, an Eight with no subtype.

Fragmented personality

Mental disorders of a kind that are psychological and not physiological correlate with one or another Enneagram type. In the fragmented personality, two or three Enneagram components have been thrown together, not so much discordantly as uncollaboratively, and moreover fall well short of 100% in their composition.

Unsurprisingly, the individual who has a fragmented personality is not healthy, and exists in an uneasy relationship with society – assuming that he is not living on the street, institutionalized, or in gaol. He is deemed to have a personality disorder. This can be less a formal designation than a label of convenience to pin on those who, by the incoherence of their behaviour, defy being categorized under a recognized psychiatric heading. Whether he can be treated is open to question. It is not to be inferred that a personality disorder is exclusive to the fragmented personality. What attitude society should adopt towards those seen to have a personality disorder is a subject of contemporary debate in the U.K.

Barry George was sentenced to life imprisonment for shooting dead the BBC television presenter Jill Dando in 1999. Psychic diagnosis shows him to have about 30% of the Five, 30% of the Seven, and 10% of the Eight.

In the fragmented personality, components of the Five and the Seven denote a nature that skims over the surface of life, in a random and mercurial fashion.

Obsessed (the Five) by an 'action-man' image and the aura of male celebrities, he made out that they were known to him and borrowed their names, as if by osmosis their fame would transfer to him. He felt nondescript and was aimless. It was not that he wanted to 'be somebody', but that he emphatically did not want to be a nobody (the outsider state of the Seven: negated). Hence the escapism of his fantasies, and his improvised 'world record rollerskate jump' in 1981, when he turned up at a stock-car racing stadium and from a ramp cleared four double-decker buses parked side-by-side – and severely injured himself.

He stalked and pestered women, photographed them as a voyeur, and sometimes assaulted them. To pester has at least four motivations: attention-seeking; a need for company; impatience and anxiety over information awaited; and an erotic fixation towards someone of a higher standing who wants nothing of it, which I believe relates to the Nine. He was motivated by the first-named two, via the Seven component. The fourth is speculated on, but not borne out by the haphazardness of his fixation on women: some 2500 photographs of 419, and notebooks containing addresses and car registrations, were discovered in his flat; and of many hundreds of newspapers removed in searches, only eight prior to the murder featured Dando.

A teacher at a special school which he attended recalled that "He didn't have conversations, or ask what anyone else thought: he just told you his views." As someone devoid of social skills (the Five), his desire to make contact (the Seven) is stalled by his manner. He is a self-centred dreamer (the Seven) who is neither a loner nor a mixer. He was found by a psychologist to have narcissistic personality disorder, which is a reasonable diagnosis of an adult acting like an attention-seeking child who tugs persistently at the sleeve of a parent, exclaiming "Look what I can do!"; histrionic personality disorder, a condition of overly dramatized behaviour -despite having an 'excessive rigidity' of feeling; and paranoid personality disorder: he had once been stopped and searched, but told the psychologist that this had happened to him 350 times in one year. To exaggerate by picking a 'fact' out of thin air is a trait of the Seven, who in doing so may or may not be a fantasist but is not paranoid – nor could the attention-seeker be so. Paranoia is examined in chapter seven.

By no means everyone is convinced of his guilt. The crime was premeditated; he can not concentrate – or therefore organize – and has poor dexterity.

On an evening in 1906, during a show at the rooftop theatre of Madison Square Garden, New York, Harry Thaw approached the architect Stanford White and fired three shots, killing him. Making no attempt to flee, he gave as his reason, "because he ruined my wife."

Thaw has about 20% of the Four, 20% of the Five, and 30% of the Seven. He was motivated not, as reported, by jealousy (the Three), but by a sense of idealism (5-4) which had been brought down to earth by disillusionment (the Four).

His wife Evelyn had met White when working as a

25

chorus girl of sixteen, and learned of his dislike for Thaw. White seduced her, and groomed her in how to dress and present herself in society; she completed her schooling at his expense. He won the trust of her mother as a chaperone and father-figure. A year later Thaw fell in love with Evelyn, and they married in 1905.

He had high-flown notions of innocence and purity in a woman (the Four and the Five respectively); Evelyn was, to him, their embodiment. These notions were subverted by the Seven component: he enjoyed whipping adolescent boys and girls. When Evelyn confessed to him that she had been seduced by White, he burst into tears and paced the room, bemoaning what she had told him.

With components of the Five and the Seven, he too skimmed over life, and with the same naivety as Barry George. He was a playboy and dandy (the Seven), with a habit of striking odd poses, and was twice interned in an asylum for years on end. His father had left him and his mother a vast inheritance.

When components of a fragmented personality adjoin each other, they should not be mistaken for type and subtype.

Incompatibility in relationships

Traits that impact negatively on relationships are, in the Two, an undue neediness or demandingness; the desire to tie the partner to the home more than he or she is comfortable with, or more than is practical from the standpoint of the partner's job or outside interests, a pleasing relationship being for the Two one in which much time is spent in domestic togetherness; disrespect for the partner's space, e.g. barging in on a conversation or period of rest or quiet; or romanticized conceptions.

Emotional and social detachment in the Five is covered under various headings in chapter seven. Above all, he should not act without informing or consulting the partner, and especially so if the latter is a Two or a Six.

In the Six, negative traits are possessiveness and/or suspiciousness; over-commitment to work, as with a home-centred Two and a work-centred Six; a partner who is unstraightforward or reticent: an insecure Six worries – and may be accusing- over what is being withheld, and why; testing a relationship to see how safe it is – until it breaks (self-sabotage); being made to feel second-rate; not being stood up to by a partner who is over-compliant (absence of boundaries); or ambivalence, in wanting the relationship on one count but not on another. To find flaws in the partner where there were none before might be thought to be a trait of the Four, but the Six should be considered first.

Freedom of movement is restricted for the Seven by a partner who is possessive or demanding; and he can feel that to be committed to one partner is to lose out, or to condemn himself to boredom. In communicating, he should stick to the facts without exaggeration or evasion.

An evaluation of the dynamics of dominance and submission, or of dependency, can be made. As an example, when a Two forms a relationship with an addict, both acknowledging the state, if in time the addiction is conquered can the Two make the adjustment from dependence by the partner to an equilibrium of dependence? And what part do they perceive each other as having had in the recovery?

There are two ways in which an Enneagram finding can be authenticated with almost complete certainty.

One is by a competent psychic.

The other is by dowsing, as in the use of a pendulum.

My understanding is that, given sufficient experimentation and practice, dowsing is within the capabilities of some 20% of the population – thus, a sizeable number of people.

On reaching a definitive conclusion the specific function of each of the Enneagram points identified should have been determined, otherwise the finding may be garbled.

That said, the true Enneagram is in a fledgling state of study, and a perfect result should not necessarily be hoped for – as the reader will observe from my own conclusions in Appendix No.4.

Chapter 3

TYPE ONE: VIRTUE/DUTY

Orientation: Towards
Outsider state: Separated. Abandoned and lost: need to be guided
Primary resonance: TYPE SIX
Secondary resonance: TYPE NINE

1-9:   Virtue and duty are generalized throughout, and condition, the whole being. Guidance comes from timeless truths, and the authority and call to obedience that they embody. Ethical (the One) and fundamental (the Nine) values are one and the same

1-2:   Virtue and duty shape responsiveness to the needs of others, which can extend to propagating religious belief. Guidance comes from conscience and the demands of social betterment and justice, as a good in itself

Comment on name of type

The names given to the One are the Perfectionist and the Reformer. Neither of these conveys accurately or comprehensively its nature. One of the many difficulties faced by students of the Enneagram is terminology. As has been established in the psychological theory of the primacy effect, first impressions count for much. The name that is arrived at for a type may therefore be decisive in determining the student's understanding of that type. Whatever name is chosen, it should be applicable to the type overall, whether healthy or unhealthy: duty may be well-founded, or pathologically deluded, or of a quality anywhere between these.

On coming into life, the One enters a school of reality: he has to make the best of – and to do his best in – the circumstances as they are. Some of them may not be what he would have wished for, or his path may seem to him to be largely dictated. As the realist that he is – and however true or warped his perspective on reality may be –, perfectionism is an ethereal aim that falls outside his range.

Perfectionism is discussed in later chapters as it arises. The trait is mostly either idealistic (the Four) or technical-creative and absolutist (the Eight). Only its neurotic manifestation might relate to the One (or the Six), in performance anxiety.

The perfectionist does not take for his starting point that which is defective, nor freedom from censure for his aim, as does the One. The type's standard of excellence amounts to striving, not perfectionism. His thinking is not governed by "how things could be" (the idealist), but by "how things should be" (the practical improver).

As to the Reformer, this is a name that has more in its favour, except that reforming influences are also attributable to the Five; and it has to be said that many Ones have enough of a task in reforming themselves. The One as reformer is motivated by natural justice or fairness, with the objective of the right ordering and administration of living.

Outsider state

For all the types, the outsider state is a physiological shadow of the person which has to be transcended for healthy functioning to be achieved. In the One, the state is perhaps the most extreme of all. Someone who is both abandoned and lost is hopelessly anxious and bereft. He can not but conclude that his situation is his own fault: he is lost because he has caused his own abandonment. Fault is an ever-recurring theme for the average or unhealthy One, whether finding fault with himself or others.

The following is the beginning of a statement recorded long ago – hence the archaic style – of a patient under psychiatric care, a One disintegrated to the Four: "I am the unhappiest man in the whole earth; my life is the gall and bitterness and bond of iniquity. I feel to be under God's condemnation. I have no comfort in rising up or in sitting down, in going out or in coming in. I can not eat without condemnation. I desire to eat and to drink to satisfy the cravings of nature, but when I partake of God's good creatures I feel it is without God's blessing." The statement ends with the conviction that "I am doomed to everlasting perdition."

Recognition of the need for guidance is inherent in the symbolism; but for someone who is abandoned and lost, from whom and from where is guidance to be had? Here we have a hint of the interiority of the One. The separative state is such that the remedy must incorporate an unbreakable link to life; the device that does so is faith.

Faith

So far as the One is concerned, faith has two expressions. Both have in them more of attitude than of action, so distinguishing them somewhat from other expressions of faith, not least in the Six.

On an exalted level, the faith of the One manifests itself in the strength to stand firm and not to cede ground in conditions of adversity and conflicting authority; the meaning of this latter term will be apparent in the two examples below.

In everyday life, his faith is tested when he is burdened by a state of affairs from which by obligation he can not withdraw, and he doubts how much longer he has the capacity to endure it, and whether a positive outcome can result.

Thomas Cranmer is 1-9. With his associates, he instituted liturgical reform in the Church of England. Their intentions are contained in the preface which he composed for the first English Book of Common Prayer, to be found under the heading 'Concerning the Service of the Church.'

In its opening words the passage carries a note of the reformist One: "There was never any thing by the wit of man so well devised, or so sure established, which in continuance of time hath not been corrupted." A standard of right observance for "this godly and decent order of the ancient Fathers" was to be introduced, from which the false, uncertain, altered, and superstitious would be eliminated, as would local variations of usage. As someone who was conscious of defect yet undogmatic, Cranmer worked to define the rules by non-compliance with which defect could be judged.

On the accession to the throne of Mary I, Cranmer found himself in a position of testing and trial where, as a One, he could either stand firm in his faith or weaken; he was to do both. He believed that what the monarch ordered must be obeyed, which meant in logic accepting the Counter-Reformation – and with it the undoing of much of his labours. He was martyred as a heretic, having stood firm in disavowing his recantation.

Thomas More is 1-9, with an admixture of the Five. Themes of the One that run interwoven through his life are law, justice, hierarchy, and order. Religion was, for him, governed by law. He prayed, fasted, and wore a hair shirt. He obeyed and paid homage to his father, even kneeling before him as Lord Chancellor. On the scaffold, he proclaimed that he was dying "in the faith and for the faith of the Catholic Church, the King's good servant and God's first", having been unable to acknowledge Henry VIII as supreme head of the Church.

Several features in him point to the Five (both subtypes):

the diversity of genres in his literary output, *Utopia* with its keynote of reason and concern with social issues, and the unfinished *History of King Richard III*. His originality is also a departure from the norm; the healthy One is thorough, methodical, and deliberate, but not original as that would leave him without the comfort of authoritative support.

Other virtues

In its complete definition, virtue is "Conformity of life and conduct with the principles of morality; voluntary observance of the recognized moral laws or standards of right conduct; abstention on moral grounds from any form of wrongdoing or vice."

The four natural cardinal virtues are justice, prudence, temperance, and fortitude. With some qualifications, all are peculiar to the One.

Justice can be viewed as having two aspects: the satisfaction of the law, as the law stands; and the harmonizing of dispute, or the redressing of defect, between the parties. In the first category, it is the letter of the law that is served. The emphasis is on the offence committed, the weight of evidence, and the sentence. Scope for judicial variation is limited. As a point of curiosity, legal precedent is a custom of the One and Nine in combination, being a source of guidance preserving of continuity.

To elaborate on the idea of the law, in language that fits the thought patterns of the One, human law is not without prejudice, nor even perfectible, because of human failing. What to the philosophically-minded is karma, or divine law, is unerring, because it can not go astray. The distinction between human law and justice is as between the law as it is and the law as it ought to be. Justice is the guiding hand of the law.

The second category of justice introduces the notion of fairness or reasonableness. Fairness gives due consideration, and is free from bias; justice based on law does not automatically have either of these properties. The difference is summed up in the term 'fair hearing'.

As a universal right, to the One justice is the remedying of what shames the conscience by its inadequacy. It does not have to do with inequality, in the sense of claims of entitlement to rights comparable to those enjoyed by others, which relates to the Six. In practice, human rights could be the province of either type, and may lead to improving the law as it stands (the first category above).

Prudence, or practical wisdom, is the virtue that keeps the One to the straight and narrow path, within the bounds of what has sanction, instilling care and economy. Prudence is also present in the far-sighted Five, and in the Six who is cautious where the motivation is one of security.

In ancient times, prudence was the virtue of the reason, on which depend the moral virtues which were posited as justice, courage, and temperance. It is prudent to be just in one's dealings so as to preserve social harmony and personal integrity, this latter being not of itself a virtue but the stance of self-confrontation and firmness by the virtuous person when put to the test; and the unjust ruler may cause opposition and be overthrown. How courage is reconciled to prudence is not clear (see below).

Temperance, or the moderation of the appetites and evenness of nature, is to the One a safeguard against things going out of control with consequences that can not be reasonably accounted for. The virtue is shared by the Five who has an aversion to excesses of behaviour or takes care over his diet (see 'Moderation' in chapter seven).

Fortitude is compounded of faith and/or hope, and the strength to endure. This is the virtue of the martyr (see 'Faith' above), and is thrown up mostly in the One, Five, and Seven.

Whilst not formally classed as virtues, two qualities that merit inclusion with them are humility and forbearance.

Humility is the recognition of superior authority or rank to that which the One has; and, for the One who regards earthly lives as a series of lessons, an awareness that he is in the role of student – however elevated he may be – to whom sources of wisdom are there for the searching out. He must not let humility impact negatively on his self-worth, in being degraded into the servile. Humility is an antidote to the pride of self-righteousness, and has been described as "the virtue without which all other virtues turn sour."

Modesty is the outer surface of humility, keeping in check the acknowledgement of merit, and not a virtue in its own right. In the Five, modesty reflects the desire not to be an object of attention. False modesty is a psychological mechanism of defence (not unknown in the Five).

Forbearance is prudence in social self-control, or a non-insistence on what is due, in the One or the Five. It should be exercised freely by the One and not forced, as if he feels under duress he reacts with tension and the health can suffer.

Classical thinkers cite courage as a virtue. Courage has three aspects, however, and the only one which could be said to be a virtue is the courage of the hero (the Six) who is steadfast – and has not had to cast aside prudence. Unreasoning and precipitate courage suggests the Seven (7-6). The courage of the Six as fanatic is a vice and not a virtue.

The Platonic conception of justice accords more with the Five than with the One, as the natural order of harmony, "every part doing its own work and not interfering with the others." The conception is theoretically perfected in the Five with a minimal subtype or none.

A virtue which figures in a tenfold classification enumerated by an occultist, P.G. Bowen, is harmlessness; one of several having more acceptance in the East than in the West. Harmlessness is an extension of forbearance, with the sublimation of self-control. Is there a link here with purity as under?

Of the remaining nine virtues named by him, five are justice, charity, contentment, simplicity, and purity. Charity relates to the Two, not least in attitude; contentment and simplicity, to the Nine; and purity, to the Five. Four of them have no specific connection with Enneagram types; they are truthfulness, self-reliance, discrimination, and self-surrender. (It might be unwise to relate self-reliance as a virtue to the Eight). The adjacency of the Two and the Nine to the One is surely a structural corroboration of the density of virtues in the One.

By and large, the One is not of a nature to stride across the world stage, holding the attention and admired. A gem of wisdom inscribed in a wayside retreat shows the reason why: "Concentrate on being better than you look instead of on looking better than you are." The reader may form his own conclusions, as he acquaints himself with the Enneagram, as to the meaningfulness of this advice from type to type.

Duty

A railway notice regarding safety states: "We have a commitment to our passengers and a duty to our staff." Without commitment to do right by others, an organization can not prosper; without duty to do right by itself, it can not function. Duty gives it integrity of existence; commitment, social cohesion. Duty in the One is to commitment in the Six as the inner is to the outer. This is not, of course, to say that they do not occur universally, but that the traits characterize these respective types. For the purpose of definition they are here paired, as they are easily confused.

In his striving to do his duty, 'must' and 'ought' are the watchwords regulating the One's thinking. It is as if an unseen presence stands permanently over him, dictating the attitude to be adopted or course to be taken, and holding him responsible should he not fully succeed or diverge from the 'right' way; his conscience is a powerful straitening influence. He is his own severest judge, noting defects more than merit, and unwilling therefore to give his achievements the credit of which they are deserving. The high standards that he demands of himself, or that are demanded of him, should be realistic; the One who struggles to live up to an impossible standard overtaxes his constitution, or worse, since he can not walk away from an undertaking.

He is efficient, orderly, and tidy, and obtains clarity where responsibility attaches to what he says or does.

Time is not to be wasted: that could not be explained. The hours of the day could, for him, be transcribed on to a worksheet, on which every time-slot would be shown to have been profitably spent. In so far as he has any, leisure activities have an educational or broadening content.

Authority is looked to for instruction, guidance, and in case of insecurity, for reassurance that his performance is as it should be. Associated traits are obedience, reliability, and trustworthiness.

Keen to acquit himself honourably, when his actions have to be defended the One responds with reasoned argument, not with sentiment, in the manner of a witness justifying himself under crossexamination in court.

If he feels intolerably constrained by the self-denying bleakness of a life-pattern forced into imbalance by the duty ethos, a resentment is generated which festers, under the pressure-lid of his self-control (see heading below), increases his tensions, and constitutes emotional baggage which until discarded will prevent his moving on.

The One who succeeds in developing rounded appreciations does well, for he has had to accommodate himself to the world around him wherein all is permitted.

Ethical values

Issues such as genetic engineering, the legal status of soft drugs, animal experimentation, prison reform, and euthanasia are ones where ethical values, by way of careful deliberation and wise judgment, are brought into the arena. The impartial One is most suited to reaching a decision where the rights and wrongs of a course of action are contested or not clear, and where no guidance is to be had from the law or what has gone before. Judgment is made in faith.

An example of an ethical morass in the U.K. – to cite one country from what could be a long list – is the treatment of prisoners. Is the traditional harshness of prison conditions – harsh because reflecting society's disapproval and the law's retribution – compatible with rehabilitation? Given the high level of incarceration and rate of reoffence, in society's eyes is imprisonment primarily for retribution or rehabilitation – or even simply to rid society of the offender? To quote an ex-criminal, a prisoner has to "turn the mind round" if he is not to reoffend. How is he to do that in a climate of blame, excuse, self-pity, anger, and possible denigration of worth: traits which reinforce his resistance to change and to authority? How many prisoners are not rehabilitated due to lack of motivational activities, or to the unavailability of contact with psychologists, which would enable them to gain insight into themselves? Lengthy and isolated confinement tells the prisoner that he has been given up on; is that by default or intentional?

The ethical need does not stop at topics of contemporary debate. At a time of student protest in the late 1960s, a One who was vice-chancellor of a university had a policy towards the students comprising three considerations: complete candour, to preclude charges of hypocrisy or injustice; the motto "Never make a rule which you can not enforce; never make a promise which you can not keep; and never make a threat which you can not carry out"; and a preparedness "to negotiate till 2 a.m. if necessary." Candour contributes to straightforwardness and is an antidote to the attitude of the suspicious Five or Six, as well as having an effect in common with trust, in being disarming (see chapter nine). The realism, and absence of adversarial posture in what was effectively a confrontation, may be noted. At the height of the unrest, to allay students' suspicions of any cover-up, he did not lock the door to his rooms when he was not there, trusting that they would not run riot; his trust was justified. It transpired that his strategy towards them had earned him their respect. Someone who had a foot in both camps – his and the students' – relayed back to him the overheard information that he had been described as "straight as a die."

Lack of latitude

Recognizing his restricted freedom of choice, if such is the case, the One who is wise – or, in terms of virtue, the One who is prudent – devises a set form of approach which he comes to know as tried and tested, for occasions when as speaker he is exposed to judgment. It follows that the spontaneity of an unconstrained disposition is not natural to him; but the delivery of a solid presentation is.

One of the negative states to which the One is susceptible is worry. In the One, worry is unvarying and not shifting; he is beset and overburdened by a matter at hand, not by the uncertain or suspected: the worry of the One is to be distinguished from the anxiety of the Six. An analogy to his state is to be sinking under a weight of water, both pressed down upon and hemmed in. His worry is usually caused, and prolonged, by his unwillingness to throw a situation into disorder.

To the average or unhealthy One, a person is either on the right track, leading to the righteous goal, or on the wrong track, leading to deception; or, for the puritan, to temptation.

If his desire not to deviate from the standard becomes

obsessive, guidance from the authoritative is supplanted by a rule-book mentality, joyless in its prohibitions and too exact in its pedantry, for fear of failure and mistake.

Self-underestimation

The One who is insecure may shoulder blame that is not his alone, or where no cause for blame exists. A One in an awkward marriage assumed a karmic reason for his predicament: that he had wronged his partner in a previous life, and was being called to account in the present one to reconcile himself to her, by endurance and acceptance; in other words, by fortitude and forbearance. After many years, he was informed by a telepathic source that nothing of the sort had happened; the marriage was training him in the handling of the problematical in human relations, a field in which he was told he would be engaged in his next life.

An unfortunate side-effect of excessive preoccupation with defect in himself is that the One may make a rod for his own back. Obvious failures or censure seem to him to validate his despising of himself; an attitude which, if unchecked, undermines the self-image entirely, leaving a sense of worthlessness from which he is unable to reinstate himself.

Self-control

As a youngster, the One did what was asked of him. He did not dispute or answer back (as did many a Six!), having respect for his elders, and for the authority with which they were synonymous; that authority was his guidance. The virtue that he has the earliest opportunity to learn – and which may therefore be strongly ingrained in him – is humility.

In his everyday dealings the One can not afford to lose self-control, since out with it go order and accountability; not to speak of his guilty conscience at having done so. His suppressed feelings, as a result of righteous indignation, paucity of resources to persuade others into line – he can not be overtly forceful for fear of the consequences –, and personal frustrations, must have constructive outlets for their energies, otherwise they are internalized into a constant irritant and worry.

His instinctual and emotional needs may get in the way of his aspirations. For the One of integrity, to moderate needs is a victory for self-control; to moderate aspirations, a victory for realism.

In tabulation No.4 (see appendix No.I) it is demonstrated that the Eight, Nine, and One are the established and equilibrated triad, denoting for the One that he is centred in his being, steadfast and assured. The Nine being also a component of the triad, the quality is completed in 1-9. To be established denotes for the Nine being at peace with, and at one with, himself and life.

Authoritarian attitudes

The One may have decided attitudes to bad behaviour and the breaking of rules, ranging from the strict to the punitive. Either subtype may have scriptural teachings as the basis for his rules; their truth is reaffirmed in 1-9, and their benefit in 1-2. Regulations of a secular kind relate more to 1-2, or the Five.

In education, authoritarian attitudes also come from the Five for whom good behaviour is a testimony to sound teaching- and learning. To him, the student who behaves badly is not 'thinking straight', and his lack of balance (a keyword of the Five) does no favours to his performance, academic or recreational. The One punishes someone 'for his own good', the Five, 'to teach him a lesson'. The One's motivation is – or is made out to be – moral guidance; the Five's, conditioning for life.

If the One gives up the struggle for self-improvement, in his own eyes his failings have proved to be stronger than his aspirations. He can preserve a semblance of virtue by transferring his judgments from himself to others.

Religious fundamentalism

Two types, the One and the Six, create by their interaction the conditions for religious fundamentalism. The reader may wish to come back to this heading on reaching chapter eight.

For the fundamentalist One, behaviour is regulated by sacred teachings, the truth of which he believes has been – and will be – strayed from. To quote an Islamic historian, the religion's educational system – which is entered at the age of five and left twenty years later, and is the fastest-growing in South Asia – "seeks to purify Islam by purging it of the influence of the past few centuries and returning to the basic texts of the Koran and the Hadiths (prophetic sayings)." The leaders of the ousted Taliban regime in Afghanistan were educated by this system.

Foreign influences are, to the One, a temptation to be resisted and an encroachment to be weeded out; to the Six, they are a threat to be combated. In resolve the One is immovable; the Six is defensive and aggressive.

By his mindset, the One provides the moral bedrock for the militancy of the Six, who acts to halt deviation and restore conformity of conduct. For the One, to punish is to purify in righteousness; for the Six, to instil obedience.

The fanatic whose objectives are communal – not the loner with his own agenda – is a Six. He may be of either subtype, the more dangerous being 6-5 in so far as he goes unnoticed, and does not bend by so much as an iota in the 'purity' (i.e. uncontaminated quality: the Five) of his commitment.

Miscellaneous traits

Perception of sexuality is negative, because fearful (consider also the Five: see 'Fastidiousness' in chapter seven)

Misconceptions as to type

The One is said to compare himself with others. It is doubtful that he has reason to do so; what he does compare himself with is his interior standard of excellence.

To the One, a standard is the measure by which to judge defect; to the Five (with no subtype), it is the measure by which to judge the efficiency and harmony of sound functioning which is promoted by the eradication of what, being wrong in method, is mismanaged.

Footnote

A quality which could merit consideration as a virtue is acceptance. Possible components are faith, discrimination, humility, and 'divine indifference' (see 'Moderation' in chapter seven). Acceptance demonstrates what resignation can not.

Chapter 4

TYPE TWO: INVOLVEMENT IN NEED

Orientation: Towards
Outsider state: Negated. Unwanted: emotional abandonment
Primary resonance: TYPE SEVEN
Secondary resonance: TYPE EIGHT

2-1:   Others' needs are met by helping them to strengthen their faith in life. The cultivation of loving attitudes. Work freely undertaken as a service

2-3:   Others' needs are met by helping them to strengthen their self-belief or to reintegrate themselves to emotional health. Personal assistance and organization

Comment on name of type

There is a consensus in the names for the Two – the Helper and the Giver – and, in so far as its healthy expression is concerned, they are accurate. What these names fail to convey is the dualism of needs of which the Two is the indicator: the needs of others that he can meet, and the unmet needs that he himself has.

What might be described as the Two's scale of needs thus ranges from efforts to help those who, for lack of ability or self-belief, can not manage for themselves or bring themselves to ask for help, perhaps not even acknowledging it when given

– literally the thankless task, performed because love and conscience (or duty) dictate its rightness; to an insistence on helping, in a social takeover with the attitude of being the only one who knows what is best for someone else – and the only one capable of doing it, or of seeing that it gets done; or to a neediness on the part of the Two – a 'need to be needed' – who invents needs in others to satisfy his own, or whose behaviour is parasitic and wreaks havoc in the lives and relationships of those affected. The categories of insistence on helping and neediness may be fused into one.

Within these extremes lie many variations, all of them having to do with a shifting balance between help needed, help given, the degree of its acknowledgment and any sense of entitlement that the Two may feel, and the benefit accruing to him by way of growth in spirit – thankfulness for the offered opportunity–, esteem, or in tangible form.

Involvement is fundamental to the Two, who is the helper or giver with a human face or on a personal basis, not the philanthropist or anonymous donor, and best appreciated by his physical presence. By his closeness, the perceptive Two can gauge how much help is sufficient yet not excessive, and is aware of what the genuine need is, should this not tally with appearances or what is said; too much help would create dependency which, in being a hindrance to growth, goes against the Two's role (see 'Love in relation to life' below). Most importantly, the Two's worth is validated by involvement, both in the need for, and success of, what is undertaken. Put simply, making others feel better about themselves makes the Two feel good.

Outsider state

To be unwanted is the outsider state of the Two; to be abandoned, that of the Six. At first glance they may seem much the same, and indeed in assessing someone from an inharmonious or broken family background it may not be possible to establish for sure into which of the two categories to place the subject. A child may be, or feel, unwanted because differing from how he or she was expected to be (the Two or the Six); or a circumstance may supervene to force his or her abandonment despite still being wanted (the Six). A feeling of abandonment caused by the affections of a parent being split between the family and a partner elsewhere would point to the Two or the Six; the death of a parent, to the Six; the absence of a parent in the line of business, to the Six; and absence due to a parent being in gaol, again to the Two or the Six (for which a Six's sense of abandonment is self-explanatory; a Two might say to himself, "If I were really wanted, he (or she) would not have acted in a way that has left me deprived by landing him (or her) in gaol.") The Two as a youngster may feel unwanted, having had every material advantage – a generous allowance, sent away to boarding school to receive the finest education, but not parental love.

It is not the fact of being unwanted or abandoned that applies, but a negative acceptance of the fact, or a sense of being so.

To be unwanted is to be emotionally distanced, disliked, or – where needs are the standard – to have failed to satisfy: not to be pleasing, obliging, or compliant enough. To be abandoned is to be separated from, by the breaking of ties, loss of allegiances or identity, or the opening up of physical distance. It is the Six who is looked down on, ignored, or shunned.

The outsider state of the Two has by its nature a personalized quality: the judgment that he is unwanted can not be divorced from sentiments towards the one who made it or acted as if it were so.

Love in relation to life

Erich Fromm finds that love "is not primarily 'caused' by a specific object, but a lingering quality in a person which is only actualized by a certain 'object' a passionate affirmation of an 'object'; it is not an 'affect' but an active striving and inner relatedness, the aim of which is the happiness, growth, and freedom of its object."

Motherhood as an ideal illustrates both the Two and the above quotation. The mother is the source of unconditional love, warmth, and safety, the emotional bedrock of the family's wellbeing, looked to for the provision of sustenance, and whenever needed for lending a helping hand or a sympathetic ear. Her kindness, support, encouragement, and interest contribute to her children's happiness, growth towards adulthood, and freedom in the wider world.

2-1 affirms love as the reality of being, in faith and hope. The subtype feels blessed and humbled by the gift of life. In the words of the First Epistle of John (4:19), "We love him, because he first loved us." The impulse that inspires 2-1 to action is the desire to relieve the oppressed in spirit: those for whom life is not a gift but a burden.

There can be a gentle, sweet, and tender side to 2-1, and a diffidence compounded of humility and a touch of self-doubt- traits which distinguish it somewhat from 2-3.

A church congregation comprises, in its heart, the Two (2-1), the Six (6-7), and the Seven (7-6), so uniting faith or belief with love.

The author Gitta Sereny is 2-1. She is driven in her investigations of individuals who are popularly labelled evil by the belief that even those who commit unspeakable deeds have not been born evil so much as made so by perverse social and environmental factors, and can be shown to contain a residue of goodness. Whether her belief is sound could be philosophically debated, but makes no difference to the appeal of its rationale.

In an analogy of home and hearth for their warmth and comfort, 2-3 is to the flames of a fire what 2-1 is to its live centre.

Dancing and singing are manifestations of the Two's positive feelings towards life, and talents that resonate with the Seven.

Human contact

Contact with others is what engages the Two with life; without it, the giving mechanism has no function.

The healthy Two is warm-hearted, conversational, thoughtful, and welcoming; and sincerely expressive of sentiments of concern, appreciation, encouragement, hope, and sympathy. He is a born correspondent, whether in writing of personal and family news and achievements, in recording a pleasurable meeting, or sundry items which it is felt will strike a sympathetic chord. As in the Six, contacts on a neighbourly and community level are extensive, reinforcing the Two's image as someone who can be turned to in need.

In the average Two, the conversational is replaced by the chatty, and the tenor is self-centred: having enquired about the other person or commented on the news, talk reverts to himself. Issues are personalized by being coloured in the mind by the personalities associated with them, and by the Two's reaction of like or dislike to them. If he is undiscriminating in gradations of social familiarity, his language is too intimate or colloquial. Social pride has him insinuating into his conversation the names of famous people with whom he has had dealings; and if he can say that he is on first-name terms with them, so much the better.

A reviewer of a biography by a Two who was married to a prominent political figure is of the view that the book reads like a family letter, and asks why "someone who has an interesting few thousand words to write about somebody else" chooses to write "several hundred pages on herself."

Meeting others' needs

Personal relationships are of overriding importance to the Two, in the scope that they afford for growth in harmony. The Two's happiness and emotional wellbeing are founded on meeting the partner's needs and adapting to them, words and acts of appreciation by the partner – renewing the desire to please –, and his own needs being met without asking. The temptation to interfere or to control must be resisted (see 'Over-involvement' below).

Determining criteria for 2-1 include the desire to please the partner, and the disparate desires and obligations to make the relationship work and to do what is right; and for 2-3, the desire to please the partner and make the relationship work, and its use as a vehicle to project an impression – legitimate or not – of marital success. The attachment of the partner to home life and togetherness is a prime requirement for both subtypes ("You're never here with me!", "The children are in bed by the time you get home", or "Why don't I come with you when you go to ?"). Hidden traits of a partner of a 2-1, which would not bode well for the continuance of the relationship, are violence, and the scorning of ethical or religious values.

It may be speculated that many of those who are habitually abused in relationships are Twos (2-3) who unconsciously gravitate to partners whose perpetration of the abuse is rationalized as confirmation that the Two is needed and should therefore stay. The Six who stays in an abusive relationship is governed by notions of security and belonging ("Where else would I go?"), or by the fatalism of 'better the devil you know.' "My place is with him" could be either the Two or the Six speaking.

Except by its motivation, the closeness of a Two to the partner may not be distinguished from the supporting role of a Nine who lives in the partner's shadow.

Bangladesh is 2-1, and home to the Grameen Bank.

(This is not to say that the bank is itself 2-1). The bank is a pioneer in the granting of microloans to the landless poor, in a social experiment which has been resoundingly successful. As at July 2000 it had some 2.3 million borrowers, more than 90% of them women; the Two is of a feminine nature, just as its polar opposite, the Eight, is masculine. Loans average the equivalent of US$ 160; the repayment rate is 95%. If one person in a syndicate can not repay, the debt is taken on by the others. The bank provides services – which do not stop at loans – in more than half the villages of Bangladesh.

Features of the One and the Two are the weaving of the bank's activities into the social fabric, in response to the need to relieve poverty; the recovery of dignity, and with it self-belief; the moral obligation of the borrower to repay; and – above and beyond all of these – faith in human goodness.

The Salvation Army might be thought to be 2-1; in fact it is 1-2, the subtype being heavy. Its ordained ministers vow "for Christ's sake, to care for the poor, feed the hungry, clothe the naked, love the unlovable and befriend the friendless." Individuals and organizations which espouse these values are helpers of last resort, endeavouring to convert the hopeless into the hopeful; faith being the strengthener of hope. To labour on behalf of the despairing and destitute does not appeal to 2-3, the task being never-ending – the Three is result-orientated – and having nothing of status.

Counseling is an occupation to which the Two (usually 2-3) may be drawn. The person who visits a counselor is the protagonist in his own drama – whether or not he has written the script. The Two, for whom life is a drama (see tabulation No.1 in appendix No.I) is present not as participant or spectator, but as witness and enabler.

Counseling should not be confused with psychotherapy, a profession of the Five which employs techniques to retrain and redirect a person's thought patterns.

Sympathy and concern are the traits brought to bear

by the counselor. In this context, sympathy would seem to be an aspect of love, a readiness to engage in situations of emotional need and, to use Fromm's term, not an affect; it is noticeable that the formal definition of sympathy – 'the quality of being affected by the condition of another with conformity of feeling' – does not accord with this mode of its expression. The counselor notes the feelings of the client; whether they are identified with, or even whether they make sense, is immaterial. Concern for the client's wellbeing is the only stake that the counselor has in the matter.

Whilst symbolically the counselor is witness to a drama, his actual function is one of encouragement, by listening and waiting, questioning, restating – the client may not register all that is exchanged, and may be unclear in what he says – and reformulating, as further detail emerges. What technically takes place is the recognition, prising loose, and dissolving of an emotional blockage. The client's problems are dissected and understood by him, at his own pace and in his own fashion. It is not for the counselor to offer a solution out of nowhere; and if he thinks that he has insights they should be held in reserve, as they could be seized on regardless of merit or prematurely by a client who is impressionable and eager for a resolution.

A golden rule in counseling is that the client must not be influenced by interference, a predetermined agenda, or coercion as to the route that the sessions take; he is being helped to help himself, not having the job done for him. As the number of self-accredited counselors has grown, some spectacular abuses of the rule have tarnished the good name of the profession. The foremost reason why this is so is that a counselor who is himself emotionally needy lets himself be caught up in the drama as a means of replenishing his emotional deficit. He thereby secures his 'fix': for substance abuse read client abuse. Incidents recounted by the client are emphasized or sensationalized by the counselor – always a redundant exercise, as the genuinely sensational speaks for itself; fanciful ideas are planted in the client's mind; and – to complete the emotional conspiracy – the counselor aligns himself in agreement with the by now parroted responses of the client.

In the media, the Two as agony aunt (or uncle) is a convenient and youthful brand of counseling. Contact with her has no closeness and is anonymous, akin to buying a packet of condoms from a slot machine instead of in the shop. Advice is given, practical and educational, and she can permit herself to be sympathetic – in the formal definition of the word – or judgmental. The reader of the magazine or caller to the radio programme can ask questions of the utmost intimacy, which the Two as a skilled counselor does not balk at answering comprehensively.

With some provisos, the post of personal assistant is suited to the Two, who should be keen to please the boss and might learn to read his mind. However, the boss of a 2-1 would have to act ethically and transparently – as would the business – for harmony to prevail; and the Two with a heavy Three subtype who could do the job by rote might be ambitious for career development. Dislocation would ensue with the departure of a Two who had taken on extra work and become relied upon; or one who, in deputizing for the boss, had improved on his performance.

The Two abounds in professions which make people feel good about their appearance; in social administration; and in advisory or self-help bodies that are women- or family-targeted.

As carer to the elderly or disabled, the Two attends to what the person can not do for himself: helping him to move around the house, cooking, cleaning, laundry etc. If domestic neglect is evident, the Two should be wary of trying to do everything, since the needs are essentially one-way – a far cry from the ideal of mutual benefit – and acknowledgment of their being met could be sparing ("He didn't even thank me"). The Two who, as a regular and loving presence, helps the mentally disadvantaged towards social integration has a One subtype.

Doing what has been left unfinished by others is a trait of the Two who has a habit of keeping busy, recapitulating the early phase of motherhood when someone has to restore the home to tidiness by clearing up the toys, clothes, and mess of every sort.

Confessional television series as a format are on the borderline of meeting a need, being characterized in the main by drama (2-3), argumentation and provocation (the Six), and the offloading of blame (2-3 or the Six).

From time to time government ministers who are Twos voice initiatives of their own, which are picked up by the media and backfire when the charge of being patronizing and bossy is levelled against their originator. A recent idea, in alarm at the incidence of anorexia, is that photographs of 'impossibly thin models' should not be paraded in newspapers.

Many prostitutes are 2-3, the 'oldest profession' being one of meeting sexual needs. Domestic premises would be natural to the type.

In a resemblance to the Six, 2-1 can overcommit himself. If he is reluctant to decline requests for his help, feeling duty-bound (the One) to give it and guilty at disappointing (the Two), he may end up with nervous exhaustion, and has to cultivate a thicker skin if he is not to be imposed on.

A sinister side of meeting needs is the collusion of the Two in the nefarious activities of a partner whose affection and retention is the Two's sole interest. Rosemary West, convicted of ten child murders in collaboration with her husband Fred, is 2-3. The psychological clue is to be found in the outsider state of the type: unwanted. A minimal Three subtype could be inferred; hers is about 10%. She had no expectation of being desirable to a man; in an early letter to Fred she wrote, "It just seems queer that anyone should think so much of me." Having met a man who did want her, nothing short of force majeure was going to separate her from him. It is surmised by criminologists that she was the dominant partner, but that is argued against by the lightness of the Three subtype, and is to overlook her exceptional passivity as a child. She is thought moreover to have had an incestuous relationship with her father – and she escaped the beatings that he meted out to the rest of the family. As a prostitute while married, she would boast not that she could satisfy any man (dominance), but that no man – or woman – could ever satisfy her (submission). The truth is that Fred, as a deviant Seven, had a sexual-sadistic compulsion in which she compliantly joined: her pleasure was to please him, in doing as he wanted, and as he did.

Rosemary West's collusion was active; it has to be wondered how much domestic abuse of children is perpetrated with passive collusion, the partner not participating but not speaking out either, 'loyalty' to the abuser cancelling out responsibility to the child.

The Six who has an overwhelming need to belong and a corresponding fear of abandonment could also be collusive. Such a person would probably have a history of being treated like a social outcast, as if stigmatized but with no wish to live up to the image in becoming a rebel.

Pride

For the Two, pride derives from a mixture of competence, appearance, and achievement. Its healthy expression is not condescending, having more of self-respect than of self-esteem, and an appreciation of social worth that in behaviour, manner, and association is avoidant of indignity and that which cheapens – or reaps the consequences if not. If he is in a relationship, the partner is held accountable likewise.

Actions to which an unfavourable motive could be

imputed are deterred from, with the reasoning: "If I were to do that I couldn't face them, knowing what they would think of me." Or in frustration he may explode, making a spectacle of himself and feeling thoroughly guilty and ashamed for days after, reflecting: "What on earth must they think of me for having behaved like that?"

Several types can show themselves up: the Two, in demeaning himself as above; the Four or the Five, in being ignorant of the social norm; the Five who is caught unprepared; and the conformist Six who, in going against the flow without realizing it, is 'out on a limb'.

The Seven may show himself up in going too far, but if so minded he can make light of it with self-deprecation.

Over-involvement

Insufficient autonomy arises from feeling unvalidated as a socially functioning entity without obtruding into the space of others, and taking possession of a portion of that space. The over-involvement for which the Two is legendary is social interference, ostensibly in a helping role; a form of being held to ransom, in which it is not money that is demanded, but acceptance of the need for, and worth of, what the Two has to give. Apart from the pejorative subtext – the interference is a disparagement of the abilities of the one who is to be 'helped' –, the offer can not be turned down without repercussion. Within the close-knit circle of family and friends, the Two has the weapon of emotional blackmail to still any protest, as in: "I owe it to you to do something for you, after all that you have done for me"; or: "I have the experience, and I've nothing else on at the moment"; or: "If I do it for you, that will avoid your having to pay for it." One way or another, the other party is made to feel beholden, and if he wishes for a peaceful life and for ties of family or friendship to stay intact, he will give in.

Unless motivated by anxiety or guilt at being in no

position to help ("I can't just stand by and do nothing"), to be over-concerned is a sympathetic indulgence and dramatization.

Taking centre stage unwarrantedly implies a fairly heavy Three subtype; as does upstaging, which displays the same insistence on socially monopolizing, and is additionally competitive and disrespectful.

Over-involvement by the Two has consequences which are draining of energies for those who are the object of it, and inflicts as severe damage on the harmony of the social unit as any type can.

Excessive expression

The healthy Two feels good by doing good. With deterioration in health, giving is displaced by needing, and less good done generates less in positive feelings; a lack that may be compensated for by – yet again – dramatizing. Since there is no drama without players, events are dwelled on and embroidered with all that they have of sentiment as relatable to personal cares and concerns. Over-involvement is more appropriation than imposition; excessive expression, more imposition than appropriation.

An overdone liveliness of language and manner, overwrought or effusive, is the harmless and undisciplined – if exhausting – manifestation of the trait.

When the Two is unhealthy and unstable, the drama has its star performer and is set in a reality merged into fantasy, or in fantasy alone. Examples could be the person who makes an accusation of rape, having dreamed up the episode, or who 'recovers' memories of childhood abuse that have no basis in fact. The genuineness of a life that is fraught with disasters and emergencies, about which those who have contact with the person are treated to a running commentary, would obviously be suspect. The roles answering to the pathology of the condition are victim or hero(ine).

Two types which should be discounted before assessment are the Six (6-7) who is frustrated at the loss of social standing, or at being denied it; and the Seven who is determined to win social inclusion. Either of these could be envious. The hurt of a failed relationship in which all hopes were invested could be the motivation for emotional fantasy in the Two or the Six.

Sense of entitlement

A combination of traits come together under this heading in a complex assortment, as illustrated in the following case study.

The wife of a vicar, a 2-3 whom we shall call Mrs.X, lived in a village where she was socially prominent and industrious. Her husband died when she was middle-aged, and a few years later her daughter married, the couple setting up home in another part of the country. It was shortly proposed by the husband that Mrs.X should live with them, so as not to be by herself, which she did. The tensions in the triangular arrangement soon became apparent. Mrs.X doted on the husband, and was demanding of his company. She did have social interests, but nothing to compare with the busy tempo of her years in marriage. She would interfere, and the wife was unnerved by her competence. Because she was frequently 'poorly', on greeting the wife friends would ask, "How is your mother?", as if Mrs.X were head of the family. It was evident that Mrs.X had spoken her mind, in propagating her version of the facts. The wife was apprehensive about the survival of the marriage. In the end Mrs.X was persuaded to move into a flat nearby, and visits from the family were maintained.

Analyzing this example, the Two is loath to ask for something directly, and the household as a threesome was not Mrs.X's idea; the husband (a One) felt obligated to her, for all that she had done for his wife – she had had an outstanding education – in the years before he met her. Had Mrs.X been resolved to live with them without its being suggested, this would have been her ammunition for emotional blackmail, forcing them to accept if they were to spare themselves a guilty conscience and recriminations ("How can we let her languish all alone, when we have an extra bedroom that could be hers?"). They fancied that she could lead her own life under the same roof – which for a Two is not an assumption that should for one moment be entertained (only for the Five!). As it was, the husband – who was wrestling inwardly with some matters which would comprehensively change his career path – could hardly cope with the imposition on his time and equanimity; an imposition which from many a wife would have brought the reaction, "To whom are you married, me or her?" Mrs.X's emptier and meddlesome existence with them is encapsulated in the adage 'The devil finds work for idle hands'. Her maladies were vague and psychosomatic, ensuring that she was the subject of ongoing concern and attention. Her conversations with their neighbours belittled – if not slandered – the wife, and put emotional allegiances to the test, besides inducing uncertainty in her over what a neighbour might have been told by Mrs.X.

It may not have escaped the reader's notice that there are discomforting parallels to the above in the predicament of Diana, Princess of Wales, on her engagement (see appendix No.4: the Two). The pivotal fact was seemingly left unaddressed: as a Two who would not be – and never could be – mistress in her own home, and whose access to her husband would be curtailed by his duties, with what and with whom – was she to fill the hours? In her quest for happiness (which was also the goal of Mrs.X, as the wife confirmed), her emotional intrigues split those within her orbit into warring camps. Her strategy was to seek solace and sympathy, as the victim of a state to the nature of which her sense of the romantic and the theatrical had blinded her: "If I am lucky enough to be the Princess of Wales", as she had been heard to say. It was observed that she made the remark "rather as if she were auditioning for a central role in a costume drama."

Envy

A woman who was in the chorus line of a drama society longed to be centre stage; she is 2-3. A leading actress in the troupe was the wife of her lover; she stabbed her to death. Her motivation was envy, and of a kind that could not be satisfied ("How I wish that I were centre stage like her. If I can't be so, I'm going to arrange things so that neither can she"). Had she felt: "I'll make her pay for depriving me of the chance", her motivation would have been jealousy and not envy (see 'Reactions to being humiliated or denied' in chapter five). A hairdresser by profession, she developed bulimia after the birth of her second child – no doubt brought on by her frustrated sense of entitlement – and would faint during rehearsals.

In her everyday behaviour she could be taken for a Six: insecure and obsessed with her appearance, she had a craving to be written of and applauded, could be vivacious or withdrawn, and was prone to outbursts; she had once made a scene when she failed to win a part. If the person who is envied is viewed both in a comparative way and as an obstacle, the correlation is with the Seven, who in emotional machinations – i.e. sentiments that are disguised, invented, or manipulated – can mimic the Two.

Envy and jealousy are treated at greater length in chapters five and six. Both sentiments stem from social discontentment and an overawareness of others, thus relating primarily to the Two, Three, Six, and Seven.

Miscellaneous traits

To patronize ('Mother knows best') (2-3)

Teasing; petty annoyances in general. Can take the form of picking away at a tender spot

Hysterical reaction (unless the Seven) Melodramatic reaction (unless the Six)

Conversion disorder: emotional issues are somatized i.e. converted into bodily symptoms, and manifest as sundry aches and pains or minor loss of function. Can arise instantly in response to a subject of conversation. Not identical with somatization disorder; attention-seeking is absent

An indiscriminate desire to please leads to the loss of a sense of identity ("Who is the real me?"); behavioural diso-rientation, by an emphasis on personal acceptance and rejection ("Why did he speak to me like that?" "Why have we fallen out?" "What have I done wrong?"); and the neglect of his true needs

Misconceptions as to type

Melancholy, as a fastidiousness of being, is treated under 'Aesthetic values' in chapter six. It should be distinguished from the state in the Two, which is one of self-dramatization, heightened imagery, and a sense of suffering or loss mingled with the hope of happiness. In the Four, any loss – which includes what has been missed out on – is felt to be one that can never be made good, and there is no self-dramatization.

Chapter 5

TYPE THREE: ACHIEVEMENT/ RECOGNITION

Orientation: Against
Outsider state: Denied. Humiliated, rejected: need to prove worth
Primary resonance: TYPE EIGHT
Secondary resonance: TYPE SEVEN
3-2:   Self-belief; achievement that stands out in degree
3-4:   Self-belief; achievement that stands out by its nature. The perspective must keep within the bounds of reality

Comment on name of type
The names given to the Three – the Achiever, the Status Seeker, the Performer, and the Motivator – are a mixed bag, and only go so far in defining it.

Achievement comes in many shapes and sizes, and by no means all of them fit any one type. In the Three, achievement tends to take the form less of a planned outcome than of a succession of results, with much manoeuvring and adjustments along the way. Recognition of achievement, and of the Three as its author, is essential to the sense of identity in its worth, for what he is seen to have succeeded in making of himself.

Someone who sets out to achieve over however long a period of time it may take, and who in the meantime receives no recognition nor seeks any, is not a Three; in stereotype he is a Five. In achieving, some types are not motivated by recognition so much as made to feel wanted (the Two), secure (the Six), accepted (the Seven), or at home (the Nine). For an Eight, the impact of the achievement speaks for itself.

To the Three as status seeker, achievement is a vehicle for advancement by influence. Types for whom to have status is less to wield influence than to be well thought of or looked up to are the Two (2-3), the Six, and the Seven.

As a name for any one type, the Performer is much too vague; and the reader is reminded that the Three is not the only type to excel in performance (see 'Assessment of type' in chapter one). Those for whom standard of performance matters are the One, in judging himself or being judged; the Three, as competitor; and the Six, within his peer group. In general, stage or screen performers are Twos (2-3), Threes, Sixes (6-7), Sevens, or Nines; and, in his own distinctive way, the Five (5-4).

A mistaken assumption is to blame for the Motivator being one of the names for the Three. The name is moreover non-specific; how could a single type motivate those of varied aptitudes, expectations, or diligence? The logic would seem to be that because he is energy driven – which he is – the Three is the one to energize others into action, whereas this is only so if he is team leader or motivational speaker. Even thus, when the Three as impassioned evangelist has the audience in the palm of his hand, excited into a frenzy of exultant empowerment – or what is fancied to be so: to the extent that he exerts control, the audience is disempowered–, how much of his performance is motivational, and how much self-promotional? Where is his core belief: in himself and his message, or in his ability to sell it?

Who it is who motivates is governed by the ends in view. The One inspires by his integrity: straight-dealing and steadfast, he can command as much respect and loyalty as the Six. The Two draws out, in those for whom it is lacking, faith in life and its goodness (2-1) or self-belief (2-3). Physical enterprise projects (e.g. climbing, trekking) are organized by the Five (5-6) or the Seven. The youth who is taught how to fend for himself, in rugged conditions and with a minimum of resources, would do well with a Five as his teacher. The Six rouses to action by his commitment. The motivator of the disaffected is the Six who, having known the same plight, has discovered how to transmute sentiments of apathy and hostility in himself, and so talks their language. An example would be the person who has experienced living on the street, is rehabilitated, and works in a scheme for housing the homeless. In education and recreation, it is the Seven who proves that learning can be fun. Sessions with him are an enthusiastic affair, laced with good humour, pertinent anecdotes, and the interestingly improvised. As motivator and perfectionist, the Eight compels those whom he is training to develop and express their talents to the utmost.

Outsider state

After he has had time to collect his thoughts, the individual who has been humiliated or rejected should reassess his situation with an inquest into why he could have failed. Was he under-qualified? Did he project himself too weakly or appear nervous (not the defects of a Three!)? Was it a mistake to hope for success, the nature of the undertaking or relationship having been wrong for him? To the Three, none of these is the reason, nor does it have to be searched for long and hard. He is indignant because he did not deserve to be humiliated or rejected. From having failed, he arrives at the conclusion that he did not sell himself persuasively enough, and in consequence his worth was not duly appreciated. In the average or unhealthy Three, this attitude casts doubt on whether he learns from experience, his intent being not self-understanding or self-improvement, but self-validation.

In ease of adaptation, and alertness to what might best serve his interest or earn him a good living, his is the most mobile of natures. He has the finest presentational skills of charm and persuasiveness, so that what he has of promise will be taken on trust. A determining issue is: what does the promise have of substance? His persuasiveness echoes the force of personality of the Eight, except that it has the object of attraction (negative polarization), and not of subjection (positive polarization).

Attributes of achievement

Belief in himself, and the confidence into which it translates in action, are essential traits of the achiever as a Three. They embody an attitude of personal enablement whereby "Things can only get better", to quote from the lyrics of the pop hit that was – not without reason – the signature tune of the incoming Labour government in 1997, with its vision of a brand new social order for the making.

Confidence is justified by achievement. In onward and upward moves, the two build up each other, hence 'Nothing succeeds like success.' The confidence of the Three has to be distinguished from the trust of the Seven, which is towards life as inherently enabling; and the Seven can be as ambitious as the Three.

The United States is 3-2, the subtype being medium. Psychic diagnosis reveals that the country changed from what it was at its birth (6-7) to 3-2 in about 1865, which correlates well with the year from which an encyclopaedic source dates the American era of industrial growth, namely 1877.

Labour sentiment as above restated the view that the American president is expected to personify the nation's 'betterness' in an inspiring way; the tone of self-importance (see heading below) is not unrepresentative.

Betterment, in this context, has to do with the defence of the values which promote the freedom and enterprise of the citizen, and his and the nation's prosperity through their material growth; and inspiring leadership, with the idea that those values are superior and held in trust by the U.S. as their self-nominated guardian. Although to be admired they are nonetheless one-sided, being centred on needs and wants, and those who – in the language of the Three – are out of the competition or not competing, have no entitlement from the guardianship.

Freedom of expression, with its subtext of insistence (shared with the Seven), and desire not to be controlled, is to the Three what freedom of thought and information are to the Five. In the Three, impression made on others follows expression, either as a consequence of achievement or – in those for whom recognition is itself the achievement – as the objective; in the Five, expression – if any – follows impression made on himself of an idea.

For the American model of achievement, the country and the world are market places, in which the indicators of success are to meet or create a demand, and size of market share. To create a demand is to cater for wants rather than needs.

In his working approach the healthy Three is industrious, organized, and result-orientated, i.e. he needs to have 'something to show for it'. He does not skimp on quality for the sake of a quick result or quantity of production, that being – with demand – his guarantee of a market. He is equal to a challenge. If he is in a business that is subject to rapid change of fashion or technology, or that is very competitive, his planning is adaptable and his market intelligence keen, so that he is not caught out by wasted investment or unsaleable stock. He is not one to struggle on in a failing venture, but cuts his losses and shapes a fresh strategy.

"It is a very American legacy: the world's largest baked goods chain, offering drivers on the move, businessmen, housewives in mid-morning and children on their way to and from school the chance to enjoy an iced doughnut and a soft drink." Thus begins an obituary of William Rosenberg, a Three and the founder of Dunkin' Donuts. By the age of 21 he was sales manager for an ice cream company. Soon he himself established a company that delivered meals and snacks to factories and offices, which grew to have a fleet of 200 lorries to serve its customers. The first Dunkin' Donuts was opened in 1950, and charged more than the standard price for a good cup of coffee. He cornered the market in high-quality snacks, expanding into some 37 countries, and was driven by the belief that "Anyone can achieve success and prominence through hard work, skill, and risk-taking."

In a competitive sport, the Three performs as his authentic self. Neither persuasiveness nor charm avails him, as they could were he a politician or in business. For him, doing ever better means self-improvement by physical and mental rigour, his success being its own advertisement. Endowment with a physical skill is rightly associated with the Three, but can occur also in e.g. the Five (5-4) or the Seven. Pete Sampras is 3-2; Nadia Comaneci is 3-4, as is Michael Schumacher.

Product advertising on a large scale is a feature of 3-2; and in a market restricted by taste or in access, 3-4. As with the evangelist in the church or auditorium, it is legitimate to ask oneself where the product promoter's belief really lies: in the merits of what he is selling – or in his powers of (self-) persuasion? If the latter, he is a born deceiver, and to have dealings with him may be dangerous. In no other type is motive harder to fathom with certainty.

3-2 goes along the beaten track and, if healthy, is like others only better. In 3-4, there is an epic dimension to the imagination. He may be a dealer in art, antiques, rare manuscripts, precious metals etc.; or he may be drawn to status and wealth in a coterie of the select and shadowy. As the artist, at their finest his compositions are on the grandest scale, dramatic and exalted. For 3-4 (but not 5-4), an expression of exaltation is jubilation. George Frideric Handel is 3-4. The breathtaking daring of 3-4 is the subtype's blessing or curse (see appendix No.4). An example from recent years is David Kim Stanley a.k.a. Michael Fenne, founder of the internet company Pixelon, who spent $16 million in company funds (80% of the subscription proceeds) on a launch party in Las Vegas. Ever-hopeful and in gaol, he maintains that he has "a unique ability to defy reality." One of his executives remarked of him, "I've never been around a cult leader, but that's the way it felt." The most spectacular of scams are those of 3-4 or 7-8.

Orientation by result

A successful result is evidence of achievement. The businessman who manufactures goods or provides a service for which demand is constant, and who updates ahead of the competition or does not have any, has an ongoing result; likewise the competitive sportsman with each win.

The average Three as national leader tinkers at the margins of an issue, more cosmetically and eye-catchingly than substantively. He may talk of fundamental reform in grandiose and sweeping language (e.g. "Tough on crime and tough on the causes of crime") but hesitates to tackle it, due to the slowness with which the result would work through, and the vagaries of planning and open-endedness of funding when long-term projects are subordinated to short-term thinking. A journalist who reported on the administration of John F. Kennedy (see appendix No.4: the Three) summed up its working mood: "A good idea is one that works. And the best idea is the one that works fastest with the least fuss while irritating the fewest people."

In the U.K., the trend to performance or league tables is an influence of the Three (the U.K. is 9-1). In education, parents can see how one school is faring compared to another.

As an outworking of a theme touched on with respect to the U.S., what the tables actually do is to enrol every school in competition, a mode geared to the student or school as high achiever. A value-added component might one day be incorporated in the tables, so that schools having a disadvantaged intake are not penalized; but to add notional value is to compensate, not to motivate. Schools at the front of the academic race can not let themselves admit those who might drag down their results; and at the back, what incentive to perform does a school have if steered clear of by the best?

As to a school's compliance with the stipulations for testing and assessment, and record of attendance, countless ways in which results are doctored have been exposed in the media.

Waiting lists in U.K. hospitals can be shortened by carrying out the easier operations, and the existence of a 'waiting list for the waiting list' has been mooted.

In those for whom results are paramount, the desire to secure them should not be degraded into an attitude of 'whatever it takes'. In the U.K., this sorry state of affairs is not helped by an administration which, in its anxiety to be seen to perform and its desire to control, has appropriated micro-management as an arm of government.

Influence and control

In the Eight, control is brought about by the wielding of superior means. Except for the Three in whom control is a byproduct of healthy growth, it is brought about in the type through imposition of personality, either by persuasiveness in conveying the attractions of what the Three proposes – a process that may be sugared for the unwilling by talked-up claims of benefit, concessions or bribery ('everyone has his price' and 'money speaks'), or the promising of more than can be delivered; or by persuasiveness in conveying his certainty of being right. The certainty may be real or apparent in its sincerity. Either way his audience is 'sold on it' – to use, again, the mercenary language of the Three, whose persuasiveness tends moreover to inequality of bargaining power. A stand of rightness can not be backed away from, should the going get tough, unless the Three is to be left roundly humiliated and without his audience.

If all else fails, persuasiveness becomes bullying. Where a relationship already exists, consequences that will be costly are threatened, or the withdrawal of favoured status.

Self-importance

A national leader who is a Three was interviewed on his government's performance by a journalist who was taken aback at the frequency with which his questions were answered "I ..." To one that was technical the response was "I'm not a scientist, but ...", and not as would be customary a summary of the data and conclusions furnished to him by specialist agencies.

Achievement is confirmed by its acknowledgment, the achiever standing out by the raised estimation of his stature. The self-important person stands out by putting himself forward and consigning all others off the stage, claiming as if by right of preemption the recognition that he presumes to be his.

When recognition of achievement is desired but not forthcoming, the compensatory mechanism is self-satisfaction ("Since they won't acknowledge what I've done, I'll do so for myself"). It may be that the actions are not deserving of recognition, e.g. they are underhand or criminal, in which case the sentiment is one of gloating and contempt.

Communication with the Three in this category is a one-way street; the agenda is his alone. He knows what is best, and listens but does not hear – an omission that is obscured under the right social graces. He is overbearing and may be boastful, which should be distinguished from the bravado of the insecure Six. His achievements are emphasized, and may be exaggerated or invented. A working arrangement with him should not be entered into without his territory being firmly demarcated. In a coalescing of self-importance and control, he neither consults nor delegates.

A blind spot can develop in his estimation of his professional performance. Rodney Ledward was a gynaecologist who was struck off by the General Medical Council in 1998, after a long series of botched operations which maimed scores of women patients. Yet he called himself "a perfectly capable gynaecologist who has done a first class job."

Primacy of image

In quality and fitness, a marketable product should speak for itself. If sold on the strength of image, either there are misgivings over whether it convinces, or it is not so much believed in, as it is a pathway to success. What is being marketed is not the product on its merits ("if this is what you need"), but its attractiveness, desirability, and promise ("you need this").

Image is the talisman of 'New' Labour. An audience is never the wiser as to how the magician performs his feat, whereas Labour's adoption of image was soon seen through; an encumbrance that can not be shaken off, and responsible for opening a credibility gap in which achievement lags behind promise, and which can not be closed by yet more rebranding and quick fixes. As a newspaper reader's letter put it, "I'd like to know how on earth can a government so engaged in media manipulation be so poor in getting their message across. Why don't they just tell the truth instead of trying to be clever all the time?"

The government should be sobered by the level of cynicism that greets its claims, in which facts are presented disingenuously. Out of a panel of 100 executives, 32 said that the administration had succeeded in its pledge to keep taxes down. In fact, under the disguise of stealth taxes the total tax burden has increased by the equivalent of 8p on the basic rate of income tax. The term 'new money' has had to be coined to denote sums invested in the public sector, after accusations of their being announced afresh more than once. Projected recruitment figures for understaffed professions are floated which are meaningless without mention of the wastage from those professions (e.g. one in three student nurses in London leaves before the end of the course).

A reliable image is one that can be trusted, not one that has to be taken on trust. With his roots in the past, the polar opposite of the Three is the Nine who, taken not on trust but on his record, is a safer bet (see tabulations Nos. 3 and 5 in appendix No.I).

Superficiality

Instead of discovering what he has of aptitudes, the Three under this heading contents himself with casting around for, and adapting himself to, whatever he can get hold of and whoever he can impress.

He communicates with the greatest of ease, and is amiable and attentive, the lack of substance in what he says passing unnoticed in the pleasure of his company. In speech and writing, the cliche and the soundbite are second nature to him. If asked to expand on a statement, he repeats himself in a patter of stock phraseology. He is never an original thinker, which does not stop him from claiming for his own ideas that he has unconsciously absorbed or consciously thieved; he can be a plagiarist.

His emotions have no more depth than his social being. An American university professor recommended one of his students for law school, reporting that "I would place him in the top one percent of the undergraduates with whom I have interacted." To a psychologist he was 'mature', 'responsible', and 'emotionally stable'. An old school friend thought that

"This guy really knows where he's going." A few years earlier, a female student had broken off their engagement, tired of his immaturity. All that had changed in the meantime was the image. The law student whom everyone – apart from his former girlfriend- rated as so outstanding was the serial killer and compulsive rapist Ted Bundy, who is a Three with no subtype.

Misrepresentation

A thoroughly likeable first impression is an impenetrable disguise. Friendly, interested in you, considerate, sincere, witty: the urbane and self-misrepresenting Three is ostensibly all of these. As was said of one, he "seemed a true charmer" and had "smart looks and good manners." The husband of the woman whom he murdered added, however, that "He was just a bit too smooth. The children thought he was slimy."

To be reasonably smooth-talking is a mark of social education; to be smooth-talking as if rehearsed and on cue is contrived. In conversation, what we say and how we say it undergo modification by feedback from one instant to the next. If this were not so, speech would be without affect or pleasure.

Integral to the smooth talk is his dexterity in having an answer for everything, in explanations and assurances, which holds the disguise intact so long as the persuasiveness of his conversation and the absence of pauses do not permit dissection of its logic.

When he expresses a complimentary interest in a woman, she warms to him and is disarmed. He is in agreement with her views. She senses that his words are tailor-made for her, and not to a formula. He sizes up the feel of the conversation for how well he is moulding her to his designs.

In any sphere, he ensures that he is shown up in the best light by adjusting the facts. What favours him is emphasized; what does not is passed over, played down, or denied. His sensational claims are believed, his self-assurance dissuading from the bother of checking.

The truth has to be teased out of a resistant Three when his misdeeds are uncovered. His composure gives nothing away. He thinks on his feet as he revises his version in order to keep up with the facts that have leaked out, or shifts his ground. He has selective lapses of memory, or conversely recalls incidents of which he had disclaimed knowledge. Delaying tactics buy him time.

As a forger, he may be less skilled than he could be, as he has his sights set on the end result and may not have the diligence to perfect his technique. It does not follow that his forgeries do not succeed, being the self-marketing type that he is.

3-4 may impersonate by taking on a self-assured identity of eminence, or at least one that invites trust.

Reactions to being humiliated or denied

In the forceful and unhealthy Three, to be rejected in a relationship evokes a reaction of outraged dignity ("How dare you reject me!"). If his manhood has been impugned, he feels an additional sense of humiliation.

Bundy began his orgy of rape and killing within weeks after having inexplicably stopped seeing his ex-girlfriend (see 'Superficiality' above). After several years their relationship had briefly resumed at his suggestion, seemingly only so that he could reject her as a payback for her having rejected him, which he had taken very badly.

Andrei Chikatilo, a Ukrainian living in Russia, was convicted of 52 murders in 1992. He is 3-4, the subtype being heavy. On being interviewed he cut a nondescript figure, having none of the charm or ease of the Three. Since childhood he had been dogged by humiliation (the Three) and shame (the Four). The family was very poor; they lived in a one-room hut. He would wet the bed, in which the rest of the family also slept, and would be castigated by his mother for doing so. Thin and weak at school, the boys in the village "called me 'Muscles'. They were always laughing at me and pushing me around... I'd cry and go into a corner somewhere ... I couldn't stand up for myself." As a youth, gossip that he was impotent went the rounds; "I was so ashamed. I tried to hang myself." Thereupon he left Ukraine.

His deviancy started with exposing himself and molesting girls; "I just wanted to show, in front of anyone, that I was a real man." He was haunted by what he had missed out on (the Four); as he recounted of one molestation, "This was what I hadn't had." His humiliation was made worse by envy linked to the sense of having missed out; as a teacher, supervising the dormitories for boarding students, "There were cases where we caught boys and girls together in bed." "I could see children doing what I had not done even when I was thirty years old." In his wanderings at railway stations and on trains, where he would watch sexual activity taking place, he was both envious and indignant.

Jealousy and envy are used interchangeably in everyday speech. One is jealous of what someone has, wishing to have it (acquisition by deprivation), and envious of what he is, wishing to be in his state (equalization). (In the sumtotal of traits of comparison, envy is at one end; at the other is admiration, which relates mostly to the Six and the Seven (7-6). A trace of admiration may inhere in envy, despite itself). The jealous person competes with the one who has what is coveted (but see below); the envious person resents him, and may or may not accept the state. Jealousy is more natural to the Three than envy. It should not be overlooked that the term 'jealousy' is also commonly applied to traits like possessiveness, suspiciousness, and fear of betrayal, all of which would relate in the first instance to the Six, and secondarily to the Two.

If (A) is a wealthy man who sounds out (B) and (C)

before making his will and (B), knowing that (A) is better disposed towards (C), sets about ingratiating himself with (A) and blackening the name of (C), (B)'s sentiment is one of jealousy. (If (B) is someone who dramatizes with fantasy, he could be 2-3). Should (B)'s schemings come to naught and the bulk of (A)'s estate passes to (C), (B)'s sentiment remains one of jealousy, even though its object is unalterably owned and so can no longer be competed for. Envy, at this point, would reflect resentment at not having a share.

Motives for revenge are humiliation or denial; to be tricked, in a deal or at gambling; contempt towards the Three; and to be sacked. A less specific motive is features of the upbringing, domestic or social, that were degrading or experienced as such.

It should be made clear that the form of revenge under discussion is motivated by indignation, as the lessening of worth, and is not the emotional reaction of uncontrolled rage by the person who lashes out in what he does.

Expressions of contempt

The Three who targets the defenceless has a self-worth that is bogus. It is not by chance that Threes outnumber any other type among the influential personalities of the Third Reich (see appendix No.6), especially Goebbels and Streicher. The role of Streicher should not be underestimated: in Alice A. Bailey's *The Externalisation of the Hierarchy* he is listed, with Goebbels, as one of "the base and dark parallel of the initiating Seven who lead human beings into light" (p. 258). Contempt that is orchestrated, as in the Third Reich, hardens into hatred.

3-4 can have contempt for rule and convention, as if it is beneath him to be bound by them. When brought to account, either he parades his humility – genuinely, or as an expedient? – or, more often, he is wordily aggrieved.

Sundry expressions of the trait are to humiliate or

degrade; brazen or taunting behaviour ("Aren't I clever to have got away with that!"); betrayal, usually out of greed; the character assassination or hate campaign; in men, hatred of women, which can be homicidal; and acts of defilement or sacrilege.

To be contemptuous of conformity or the majority view is a trait of the Six as rebel who can not in any other way validate his difference, or who wishes to be noticed.

Miscellaneous traits
Tastes are refined, elegant, expensive (3-4)
Fear of being seen as inferior in achievement, in failing or being rejected. The trait may be expressed positively, and could be very aggressive; or negatively, as in cheating: e.g. a student for whose parents 'failure' is not in their vocabulary, or a researcher whose prospective results have been talked up beyond what he can deliver
Violent sexuality
Self-pity, when pride is confronted by lack of success
Saturation campaign (overkill), physical or emotional e.g. one type of stalker; saturation bombing. Overkill is also evident in the person who uses a maximum of force at the slightest provocation, which could be a learned pattern from being brutalized
Exonerates himself by reference to conspiracy theory (3-4) False prophet; mocks cherished beliefs (3-4)
Black magic (3-4)
Blood fixation; may have a sexual connotation (3-4) Tentative only: pyromania (3-4)

Misconceptions as to type
Sexuality is in no way secondary to the average Three: he is energy driven. An issue to consider in a lasting relationship is whether it is mutually loving, or has been established as a facade to project the desired image, and in which his

emotional responses are acted out but not experienced.

The 3-4 who has a need for excitement can be mistaken for the Seven with the same need. In the 1970s, Jacques Mesrine was France's most wanted criminal. Since an early age he had craved excitement; he regarded his army service in Algeria, for which he was decorated for valour, as the most exciting period of his life. He later became a romanticized outlaw figure, robbing banks and kidnapping, and escaped from a gaol designed to be the escape-proof showpiece of the Canadian prison system. For the Seven, in contrast, excitement is of the physical senses and in the present moment. In committing a misdeed, it can be added to for both by taking steps that bring as close as is dared the risk of being caught. Sports involving speed appeal to both: to 3-4, in being dynamic ('energy-driven') and away from the ordinary; and to the Seven, for the exhilaration.

A visionary, as someone who is intent on remaking the order of things to conform to his plan, would traditionally be taken for an Eight. It may be worth recording that one of my psychic colleagues has used the term twice – in examining Threes with no subtype. In this respect, the reader is cautioned not to confuse the visionary with the idealist.

Footnote

Humiliation may be at the root of one of the traits listed under 'Expressions of contempt': hatred of women, on the part of the controlling Three whose sexuality is unrestrained. In a sexual act with a partner, his satisfaction is necessarily subordinated to the willingness of the woman – unless he is to use force, which the unhealthy Three often does. His hatred could be an expression of unconscious revenge for the humiliation (i.e. surrendering of control) experienced.

Chapter 6

TYPE FOUR: THE AESTHETIC IN ART AND IDEA

Orientation: Away from

Outsider state: Estranged. Banished into life, as if from a higher estate

Primary resonance: TYPE NINE

Secondary resonance: TYPE SIX

4-3: Representation of the aesthetic

4-5: The aesthetic concept

Comment on name of type

Of all the Enneagram types, the Four is the most abstruse to embody in concrete language, and the least understood. The type is said to be creative; undefined, what does that mean? Nor is it helpful to probe the psychology of the artist for theoretical motivation; how can it be taken for granted that artists have one solely? The Four is, in any case, as peripheral to art as to much else in life. This is not to disparage the type in the slightest, but to imply that it has its own unique setting, from where it should not be removed if its nature is to be grasped.

In a beautiful passage that speaks to the Four, summarizing what Pandit Bhagavan Das wrote on the subject of art, the theosophist K.Browning makes reference to "the metaphysical conception of the whole Universe as a work of Art, of

Self-expression, Self-realization; a Drama, a Play, deliberately planned by the Eternal Artist, Poet, Creator, Who having created it says it is good, Whom we know and feel as the Self, to Whom enjoyment includes tragedy as well as comedy, the tasting of pains as well as pleasures."

Names given to the Four are the Artist, the Tragic-Romantic, and the Romantic. Although the type may indeed be the artist, many Fours are not. More to the point, the Four as artist is vastly outnumbered by those belonging to other types. The art of 3-4 has grandeur, even splendour, and makes the greatest claims for itself. Meticulousness, perfected technique, and photorealism are skills of 5-4. The Six (usually 6-7) accounts for the bulk of modern art, being the portrayer of the contemporary; an intended – or experimental – effect is produced, and a reaction evoked in the viewer. 6-5 is more refined, and can have an element of the enigmatic, as if throwing down a challenge to the viewer's discernment. As a Seven, the artist stands out for his imaginative shaping of forms and bold use of colour; he is the artist at play. Surrealism is an art form of the Seven. No doubt this does not exhaust the range of artistic expression on the Enneagram – nor has poetry or music been touched on–, but the inadequacy of the Artist as an appropriate name for the type does not need labouring further.

As can be seen from tabulation No.I (see appendix No.I), the triad of types Two, Three, and Four has in common the dramatic, not as stage production but in the experience or expression of drama. In the Two, the interplay between the self and the events of daily life gives rise to drama; in the Three, the self is exhibited through the magnifying lens of drama; in the Four, the self hankers subliminally after an existence undulled by worldly imperfection, intense to the senses and rich in imagery beyond anything attainable in the here and now. Thus there is good reason for the Four to be called the Tragic-Romantic; but the name is susceptible to misunderstanding – Tragic-Idealist would be nearer the mark –, and of questionable recognition by those Fours who live contentedly and connectedly, and who have faced no worse dramas than their non-Four friends and neighbours. A literal interpretation of the name is to be avoided: the person in the public domain over recent years who would best be described as the tragic-romantic is surely Diana, Princess of Wales; she is, however, not a Four but 2-3. The tragic-romantic content consisted of her unrealized expectations of happiness coupled with the scale of public affection towards her. Her perspective was too romanticized, not too idealized as would be the case for a Four. The Romantic is a name that could relate to the Two or the Seven.

Aesthetics, derived from the Greek word for perception by the senses – as opposed to thought –, was first defined as the criticism of taste, then by Kant as 'the science which treats of the conditions of sensuous perception.' Its use in the context of the Four is examined under the heading 'Aesthetic values.' This chapter will not cover the theories as to the causes and modalities of aesthetics, since they would relate to the Five. The abundance of such theories, together with the varied meanings of the terms, may be telling us that the subjective nature of aesthetics does not lend itself to the scientific approach. Would an artist, conversely, depict a mathematical formula? And what purpose would that serve?

Several considerations raise doubts as to the explicability of aesthetics by the elaboration of a theory. Two of the components of Jung's fourfold typology of psychological functions – thinking, feeling, sensation, and intuition – are engaged in the aesthetic process: sensation, as the function of sensory awareness, factual and undisputed in its registering of form, colour, sound etc.; and feeling, the function of appreciation and value judgment, recording an impression that is either pleasing or displeasing to a given person, at the time and in the circumstances ruling. Yet an aesthetic experience is accessible to someone who has thinking for his primary psychological function, and for whom sensation and feeling are relegated to auxiliary and inferior function respectively.

Kant postulates a harmony between the imagination and the understanding of the viewer (or hearer). This presupposes that the viewer has simultaneously understood the experience, which in Jung's typology is untenable, thinking and feeling being at opposing poles as positive (thinking) is to negative (feeling), and incapable of operating in conjunction. It could be added that enjoyment is not something to be understood, being pleasurable (feeling) and not reasonable (thinking).

Some theorists attribute value to the 'aesthetic object'; but the value invested in it, by projection of the feelings of pleasure, is personal and incidental, and can not moreover be demonstrated.

Beauty is not identical with the aesthetic. In classical painting or the architectural glories of antiquity, magnificence is a class of beauty by enrichment; likewise the technical mastery which in its fineness of detail no photograph can equal, or which creates unrivalled nuances of expression, shading, or perspective: the beauty of formal perfection. These qualities are ones of universal and timeless admiration; as such, their estimation rests on a value judgment with which all agree, not a subjective one.

In similar vein, it is magnificence that comes to mind when we witness natural phenomena like the aurora or a volcanic eruption. These sights are precluded from being aesthetic not in being observable by anyone in the area at the time, but by the attention and awe that they command, overriding the impulse to aestheticize. The night sky is a case apart for the Four, evoking both a sense of oneness across dimensions and of measureless separation.

Outsider state

To be banished to a foreign land is to relinquish all one had that was tangible; what persists are patterns of habit and attitude, and memories. The person who is banished finds himself on fresh terrain, where these patterns have no significance; but unless prevented he is drawn to perpetuating them since they are what is familiar to him. The Four is a lone immigrant to a land well populated, and has to interact if he is to thrive. The symbolism is apt: the Four is by far the least widely distributed of the types, which is why in this chapter its traits have had to be illustrated for a large part by reference to 5-4. He encounters barriers in communication and adaptation, which he does not surmount more than he is obliged to. Ignorant of the ways of his new world, he is naive, and exists largely within himself; in the terminology of Jung, he is introverted.

For the Four, banishment into life is a rude awakening into coarsened conditions, about which he is unenlightened. He has a nostalgia for the rarefied intensity of his life before, but the knowledge of it is gone, only its quality remaining, which he yearns to recreate in actuality or imagination. He is anachronistic and culturally fastidious, and his everyday notions are high-flown. How he succeeds – or fails to succeed – in adjusting to normality is the motif of the type.

Aesthetic values

Aesthetic appreciation has two forms: the creative or active, and the contemplative or passive. Both are explored under this heading.

Taste is defined by Kant as "the faculty of estimating an object or a type of idea in respect of satisfaction or dissatisfaction without any interest. The object of such satisfaction is called beautiful." 'Without any interest' means contemplatively, without the mediation of the will.

Santiago Calatrava designed Valencia's City of Arts and

Sciences. Built from hundreds of laminated glass panels and of a dazzling white, the project is the largest of its kind in Europe and was ten years in the planning. It is a synthesis of the aesthetic and the symbolic, soaring and elegant. From the outside, the Science Museum makes the viewer think of an animal skeleton, a theme which he confirms is an inspiration for his work. When at night the Cinema is reflected in the complex's vast pool of water, it looks like a giant eye with lids. Given the enormity of the project, he would be taken to be 3-4 or 7- 8 but is in fact 4-3, the subtype being light. He is said to be a monkish figure.

In his struggle to represent the aesthetic, Vincent van Gogh (see appendix No.4: the Four) demonstrated the melancholy of the type, which is a fastidiousness of being and by its nature on the fringes of the aesthetic: wistful, tender, and sad. Melancholy is not necessarily a sense of what is lost or missing, but does for the most part hinge on some aspect of the Four's art or of life not being what he would wish it to be in the ideal, or on his awareness that an aesthetic experience may never recreate itself.

A concept may be aesthetic, to the person who so perceives it; he is typically 4-5 or 5-4. Paul Dirac, a theoretical physicist who died in 1984, is 5-4. For many years he was the Lucasian Professor of Mathematics in Cambridge, a post once held by Isaac Newton. He was one of the founders of quantum physics, and in the 1920s produced an equation containing the first hint of what is now termed anti-matter. The motiveless factor of chance was in play; as Dirac admitted, he did not have the courage of his convictions as to the seeming absurdity of the existence of a particle to which his equation was the signpost. On a blackboard he wrote, in words that have never been erased, "It is more important to have beauty in one's equations than to have them fit experiment." He is not alone in having remarked on the beauty of pure mathematics; and in passing, how is its beauty (and mystery) reconciled to its logic? Aesthetic concepts validate the axiom that truth is beauty.

In its conventional depiction, the Enneagram is itself an aesthetic concept, by virtue of its encompassing the sumtotal of human nature within a design so mysteriously simple and symmetrically elegant. It is the case that to demystify the Enneagram by deciphering it does not detract aesthetically from its mystery.

What might be called the random aesthetic experience is a third category. Its distinguishing feature is incongruity: the juxtaposition of the strange, rare, or unique, with the commonplace. It will be recalled that this mimics the symbolism of the banished Four, as a stranger fortuitously deposited in a land of shared sociality. The object of the experience may or may not be of human origin. Consonant with the orientation 'Away from', as for the artist the experience is solitary and not shareable – who else would appreciate it? –, and internalized by association of the object with the imagination, in a psychological compensation for what is lacking outwardly. The intensity of the experience results from the shock of incongruity to the senses. These random events are token consolations to the Four, assuring him by glimpses of an ever-present and sharper reality than what to him is the dreary ordinariness and bogus sophistication of modern living.

Incongruity may forge a friendship of aesthetic enjoyments. John Duigan is 5-4, the subtype being heavy. He directed the film *Lawn Dogs,* in which a ten-year-old girl living on an upmarket estate and recuperating from an operation strikes up a friendship with the college drop-out who mows the lawns. Their togetherness and their separateness coexist, delicate and tender in what is, and poignant and without the words for what is missing or communicated between them at cross-purposes, – until wrecked by the baseless suspicions of others too knowing for their own good.

Cultural values

Although not normally a poet, the Four values language for its wealth of expression and beauty of representation. Prince Charles is 4-5. In an address to a religious gathering, he spoke of people wondering "what it is about our country and society that our language has become so impoverished", "a dismal wasteland of banality, cliche and casual obscenity," adding that "If we encourage the use of mean, trite, ordinary language we encourage a mean, trite and ordinary view of the world we inhabit." In a milder fashion, a Four of my acquaintance told me that she dislikes the lazy repetition of the written word. Impoverishment, in the quoted speech, denotes cultural enrichment being allowed to be lost; a standard theme of complaint by the Four, who is easy game to accuse of sentimental archaism, for facing in the wrong direction to the march of the times. The fashion leader is the Six, with whom the Four is in attitude at loggerheads (see tabulations Nos. 6 and 7 (4-5/6-7) in appendix No.I). As Charles has mused, "The fear of being considered old-fashioned seems to me to be so all-powerful that the more eternal values are abandoned under the false assumption that they restrict progress." Or as one of his biographers puts it, "He has never been in sympathy with the age in which he lives."

The Four may accept the anomalies between himself and the contemporary, neither raging against symptoms of deculturalization, nor compromising himself by trying to conform, in being what he is not. In sources and materials, preference is for the primary over the derived: for the authentic over the substitute, the natural over the synthetic, the unrefined or unadulterated over the processed; and for the high quality, distinctive, or tasteful over the ordinary. Many Fours and 5-4s favour natural remedies (e.g. herbs, homeopathy) instead of drugs, and foods that are free of human intervention.

A misconception that can be disposed of at this juncture is the reputation of the Four for elitism, which is the cultivation, by submission to a regimen of rigour, of the choicest segment of cultural expression in a given field. To be counted among an elite is to be a part of, disciplined and competitive; the Four stands apart from, and whilst he can be disciplined he is non-competitive. When his achievement is acknowledged, it will have come about not by communal elitism but by a niche demand for what he has to give out.

Nonetheless, the notion of elitism does bring out a substantial trait of the unhealthy Four, that of a quasi-aesthetic exclusivism, by absorption in the pleasures of the obscure and exotic. If the bridgeable divide between himself and the outside world should thereby widen into an unbridgeable gulf, the preciousness of his self-regard rationalizes the withdrawn state as a legitimate exoneration from having to live as does the rest of society.

Sense of distinction
As a conferring on the self of a spurious and solitary worth, elitism has – happily for the Four – a counterpart that can advance and not retard him.

In the symbolism of the outsider state, the Four is both a lone voyager and out of place; he has no instinctual mechanism supplying a ready-made connection to life, and what the average person settles for, he can not. He feels himself to have a uniqueness; a quality of which he can avail himself positively, in stamping an imprint of originality on what he undertakes.

He is free of prejudices of the standard kind, having – logically – an aversion to stereotyping. He has no objection to conformity, in those for whom it is right.

Luxembourg is 4-5. Radio Luxembourg, 'Your Station of the Stars', had a unique status on the airwaves until the advent in the 1960s first of pirate stations off the U.K. shores, then of domestic commercial broadcasting. Updating to the present day, about 46% of European households receive broadcasts via the Astra satellite system, which is controlled by the Societe Europeenne des Satellites from an 18th century chateau in the Luxembourg countryside. At the time of writing, the company broadcasts some 560 television services and 370 radio services.

I find Israel to be 4-5 with a very heavy subtype (45-49%); and Theodor Herzl to be 5-4. He is the modern-day founder of the Zionist Movement.

In *Der Judenstaat* (1895-96) he wrote, "We are naturally drawn into those places where we are not persecuted, and our appearance there gives rise to persecution. This is the case, and will inevitably be so, everywhere, even in highly civilized countries, so long as the Jewish Question is not solved on the political level."

He concludes, "The world will be freed by our liberty, enriched by our wealth, magnified by our greatness. And whatever we attempt there to accomplish for our welfare, will react powerfully and beneficially for the good of humanity."

Some of this is echoed in *The Externalisation of The Hierarchy* (p.551) under the heading The Gradual Dissolution of Orthodox Judaism – Reasons:

- Because of its presentation of a wrathful Jehovah, caring only for its chosen people.
- Because of its separativeness.
- Because it is so ancient that its teachings are largely obsolete.
- Because when the Jews become spiritual they will greatly benefit mankind, for they are found in every land.

Under The Balfour Declaration of 1917, the British Mandate was set up in a way to equip Jews with the tools to establish self-rule at the expense of the Palestinian Arabs – more than 90% of the population at that time.

The Law of One teachings (Ra) tell us that "in approximately 3600 of your years in the past, there was an influx of those of the Orion group.

"They were able to begin working with those whose impression from olden times was that they were special and different."

Soon thereafter, we are told that "the intense portion of what has become known as Armageddon was joined."

Modes of employment

Undemanding Fours, or ones who are in no position to be choosy because a livelihood has to be earned, content themselves with routine employment, reserving their particular interests for leisure hours, in the hope that a job 'made for them' will come to their notice. For Fours in general, what was stated under 'Sense of distinction' above applies in so far as practicable.

Another approach is to be selective, as in self-employment or in securing a job of which there are few holders or only the one.

Any occupation in which the drama of the human condition is witnessed may draw a response, as an escape route from the commonplace, and as a conduit for the imagination and unexpressed feeling. (This is in contrast to the Two, who creates or promotes drama and expresses feeling). A 5-4 who is a nurse told me how she experiences situations which in society may never be come across. "To be present when someone dies, I think is a real privilege. In some ways it is very sad but it's also really amazing because in that one moment whatever life is, it goes from them and you can't help but wonder what happens next." In saying this she reveals the mysterious and interdimensional feel that she has for human existence, a variation on the wonderment beneath a starry sky mentioned earlier: we are not in truth alone each one of us, but of universal – and, as some Fours and 5-4s perceive, exiled – kinship, yet of what or whom that is hidden to us are we a part? The privileged nature of her job is carried into the social side, in what patients disclose in conversation with her.

Inappropriateness to life

In epochs that have celebrated culture and respected otherness, the Four would have been at home, but the type is out of sympathy with our times: with culture not as mainstay of civilized living but as fashion accessory and status symbol; a rush towards a technologized era of dizzyingly incremental information flow – with its compulsive side-effect of language mutilated; and the loss of diversity to standardization and monopoly (of which genetically-modified foods are an example). As if heritage is something to be resented as an impostor, a contemporary artist has stated that devotion to cultural achievements of past ages "disenfranchizes the present", and that "artworks are no more eternal than flint arrowheads, Latin, or flared trousers." Uniqueness is a facet of diversity, into which for the Four the indiscriminate – as of information flow – and the standardized are at best tasteless accretions, and at worst marauders and destroyers of culture.

He is not worldly-wise; the artful social skills of dissimulation and self-protection elude him, and when he is not uncommunicative he can be self-revealing. His perspective on life is idealized and wishful. Pitting the ideal against the experiential, he has to accept that the perfection of the ideal is a mental construct, and its material outworking always imperfect because not thereby originated; otherwise he is doomed never to be satisfied.

The depression and melancholy to which the Four is prone can be habitual. Their symbolic cause is a nostalgia of being: a yearning for 'the land of lost content' of which A.E.Housman (5-4) writes in *A Shropshire Lad* (poem XL):

"The happy highways where I went
And cannot come again."

From the tone of these lines it might be thought that the writer is lamenting no longer being a child, but if so that is probably an idealized memory, although it is true that he feels the loss of the insulating comforts of childhood. The Four subtype gives him a sense of aesthetic privation in having to live as an adult in the world of bland conformity that society has fabricated for itself. As he confesses in *Last Poems* (poem XII, which is a plea for the otherness of the Four and the Five to be respected):

> "I, a stranger and afraid
> In a world I never made."

Hypersensitivity is a trait mostly of the Four and the Five (5-4). In the Four it manifests as a morbid self-consciousness, as if the eyes of everyone are on him, and as shame at his social incapacity.

If the lack of adaptation is not remedied, he fancies that he has an insurmountable defect: some vital component of his constitution must be missing, or is so badly flawed that if he could he would dissociate himself from it. By this stage his attitude has degenerated into self-contempt.

At his most alienated, in his despair and disillusionment he could pose a suicide risk.

Misconceptions as to type

A majority of authorities relate envy to the Four. Envy is, however, a sentiment of comparison: the desire to be what another is, and resentment at not being so (see 'Envy' in chapter four). Why would the Four, with his sense of the uniqueness of being, feel envy? He may observe the smoother passage through life that is the lot of some, but that is a generalized lamentation. If he has unsatisfied desires, they are on a level less banal than that of envy. Or, as a mystic expresses it: "Lord, in that secret place where ever flow / the quiet waters of the timeless sea, / grant I may know the truth I longed to know / and be at last the one I wished to be."

Much of the creativity that is postulated for the Four is actually the work of a 3-4 or 5-4. Of itself and without a sizeable subtype or admixture, the Four is seldom a high achiever, because so idealizing. Its harnessing to the Three or the Five conditions the Four component to a reality in which the idealized imparts value to the whole but is not the vainly-attempted driving force.

Destroying a piece of work because it is perceived to contain an imperfection, then starting it again, is a tendency ascribed to the One.

In the first instance the Four should be considered, especially if the perception is subjective.

To be abandoned is an issue for the Two or the Six, not the Four. The Four who is in a state of alienated torment is said to be guilt ridden. Such a Four has a sense of shame, not guilt; he is ashamed that he is hopelessly wanting in worldly wisdom, or that his nature is not 'normal' in its instincts. The trait can extend to 5-4. Guilt is an inquest by the self into what are judged to be failings of character; shame is a social handicap of self-consciousness, as a state apart. Guilt is a sentiment of the One who would wish that he were able to deter himself from doing what he knows to be wrong; of the Two who feels that he/she has let others down (e.g. "I was a bad mother", or "He needed me, and I should have been there for him"); and of the Six who is caught between two courses of action, where doing the right thing by those towards whom he feels obligated clashes with doing the right thing by his conscience.

Chapter 7

TYPE FIVE: THE THINKER

Orientation: Away from
Outsider state: Disempowered. Need to regain rational control of the self and its space
Primary/secondary resonance: NONE

5-4:   Thinking is inductive, outward from the particular to the general, or from consequence to cause. A perspective that encompasses by enlargement (negatively: thinking is too loose and beyond reality). The scope of possibility

5-6:   Thinking is deductive, inward from the general to the particular, or from cause to consequence. A perspective that defines by reduction (negatively: thinking is too tight, limited, position-taking). The comfort of certitude

Comment on name of type

Of the two names given to the Five, the Thinker is to be preferred to the Observer. Both are blanket terms, but the former less so.

For the Five, thinking is his pathway to knowledge and its self-empowerment, thence to an understanding of the world he lives in; understanding arising when knowledge finds its right place within the totality of his thinking. He does not advance himself by merits of personality- that of the Five seldom shows out on first meeting, and is never advertised –

but by the worth of his knowledge and technique; this latter being efficiency and accuracy of method.

Excluded from this heading is thinking about personal issues, or ones having a content reducible to the personal, unless it is with a view to understanding their nature. Much of what passes for thought along these lines (e.g. by the Two or the Six) is actually feeling and not thinking; this is always so when a value judgment expressing pleasure or displeasure is made or implied: thought is neutral.

Brooding (e.g. by the Four who is self-lamenting; the alienated Five; the resentful or stymied Six; or the Nine who suppresses the desire to act on negative sentiments) is not thinking, being governed by mood.

The Five observes in order to learn, observation being for him an indispensable adjunct to thought. Experimentation, or the accumulation and analysis of data for consistency and anomaly, are forms of observation.

Words being the expression of thought – and not to overlook the poet and the playwright–, many of the finest novels ever written have been the work of Fives (5-4), drawn out from their storehouse in memory of observed human behaviour, without any agenda – given their detached perspective – but the truest of likenesses. (Charles Dickens, as a 5-6 (see appendix No.4), does not fall in this precise category).

Other types who make use of observation are the Three, in sizing up what serves his best interests, how he can outdo the competition, or whether he is succeeding in motivating or winning over; the Six, for security, which means either conformity – is he at risk of being out of line? –, or safeguard against a danger or opponent; and the Seven, in opening up new and perhaps fascinating avenues of experience.

To have an avid curiosity in observing is common to the Five and the Seven, the motivation being thirst for knowledge or thirst for experience respectively.

Outsider state

What places the Five apart in otherness is his free-standing posture. In this state he is adrift in life, which makes no sense to him. He does not ask himself "Who am I?" – that is a question posed by the Nine who feels no sense of identity with anyone or anything – but "What am I doing in life?" or more exactly, "What is the nature of the knowledge which will enable me to orientate myself so that I am at home in life?"

Uniquely, the type does not resonate with any other, so he can not discover himself by interaction and adaptation. Human contact is overwhelming, jars his being, and is not meaningful to him: he is a thinker. The ideas of 5-4 are over-imagined, and in their loftiness take leave of reason altogether. 5-6 views the world as if through a magnifying glass, and with a one-track mind. Both subtypes are, on this level, highly subjective, being without the experiential points of reference which would substantiate or refute the imagery that in thought comes to them.

Franz Kafka is 5-4. His novels transport the reader into the outsider state of the type. The central characters are not only adrift, but prisoners of circumstances which they have no way of understanding or controlling. 'Knowledge is power', as any Five will affirm; these characters are powerless. A symbol of the Five who is lost in his mind is the labyrinth.

A theme of disempowerment for our times is the activities of the computer hacker, which to the Five are also perceived as entry into his space.

Modalities of thought

The form of thought commonly associated with either subtype of the Five is logical: directed and on a step-by-step basis. Information is assembled, analyzed, and organized, with judgment as to what does or does not bear on the matter. Reconsideration may be undertaken at any stage ("Where is this leading?" "Are the results reliable and coherent?").

To gather data as evidence which is analyzed, classified, and systematized in support of a theory is a method of 5-6. A theory that is secure (the Six) from attack has for its foundation a weight of evidence that on rational grounds can not be disputed.

An example of the method was the findings half a century ago of Alfred Kinsey, the sexologist, who as a graduate had taught zoology and botany. He devised a 350-point questionnaire which was responded to by 18,500 Americans, to produce the most thorough survey ever of sexual practices, and overturning many a preconception. Kinsey was himself bisexual.

Cast of mind

5-4	5-6
The world of being	The world of becoming: of motion, alteration
Speculation on causes	Observation of effects
Investigation of the unseen or occult; the unknown quantity; the contemplative	Techniques of diagnosis, prescription, and treatment; the known (isolated) quantity; the technician
Natural theory	Man-made theory
The abstract e.g. pure mathematics, (moral) philosophy; the timeless in the natural world and the human condition; the poet	The contemporary or time-bound e.g. sociology, economics, history
The psychologist as free-thinker	The psychologist whose determinations are defined by theory
Theoretical foresight e.g. actuarial	Practical foresight
The ideal and the contemporary have to be reconciled	Attuned to the contemporary

5-4 is the point at which science (the Five) and art (in this context, the Four) intersect. If a science is a body of knowledge, an art as its complement is a pleasing arrangement of that knowledge – pleasing because having truth and beauty, order and harmony. Johann Sebastian Bach is 5-4; it has been said that he is to musical composition what Newton (see appendix No.4: the Five) is to science. Perfection of technique is a trait combining the exactitude of the Five with the idealism of the Four.

For professional use, the Enneagram is indicated in the first instance for 5-4, the theory being natural and discovered, not man-made and invented. An additional difference between the subtypes is that in the Enneagram 5-4 has nothing to defend, having no ownership over it. In the event 5-6 has no ownership either, but would wish to systematize his results in a fashion as water-tight – i.e. secure – as he can contrive; he has therefore to guard against a forced fit of data in the desire for conclusiveness of presentation. Other types who could be attracted to the Enneagram are the One – and again the Five for whom it is an ethical or religious framework by which to live; the Two as counselor; and the Seven, for whom the Enneagram could be a route of endless fascination and detours.

As a counterpoint to logical thought, 5-4 is also the domain of the poetic and of much that is esteemed in literature expressive of imagery created or recreated. Themes to which expressive thought lends itself extend to the absurd, the aberrant, and the monstrous.

With his poem *Strange Fruit,* Abel Meeropol (see appendix No.4 under Billie Holiday: the Six) composed a unique and powerful indictment of racism. A literary technique of contrasting images may be noted: the second verse opens with a 'pastoral scene', which in the next line is smashed with a hammer-blow of words conveying a lynching. The contrast is repeated in the next two lines. He writes from a sense of outrage, and succeeds in his message because the imagery strikes home and lingers. Had he been 5-6 and not 5-4, he would instead have written a reasoned exposition on lynching, or a polemic, neither of which would have so endured. The conclusion to be drawn is that the art of expression in verbal imagery can be of greater force than argument from the facts.

Should the reader be puzzled as to why, under 'Cast of mind' above, pure mathematics is classified with poetry under 5-4, the reason is aesthetic: a mathematical equation which expresses a natural law is the poetry of science.

Vladimir Nabokov is 5-4. In 1939 he wrote a short story in Russian entitled *The Enchanter*, about a man who marries a woman in order to possess in union her young daughter. The theme lay dormant in his mind until, having long since emigrated to the U.S., he wrote *Lolita*. He is a master craftsman of language; his style is intensely rich, a maze of layered meanings and ambiguities, allusion, and verbal artifice. His wife Vera said that in 48 years she "never once heard him utter a cliche or a banality", which calls to mind a statement by Prince Charles (4-5) quoted in chapter six. For Nabokov, a work of fiction should yield "aesthetic bliss." Thematic randomness and incongruity – the byways of the imagination: in his own words, "thematic trails or currents" -have a central role here (see 'Aesthetic values' in chapter six). In pornography, on the other hand, he declared that "obscenity must be mated with banality", and the aesthetic is forgone: banality has no byways. He admits to being "the kind of author who in starting to work on a book has no other purpose than to get rid of that book" – a motiveless act of which only the Five is capable. *Lolita* has, moreover, "no moral in tow." As a meticulous Five, he compiled a card index of technical (e.g. anatomical) details to ensure accuracy of character representation. Every summer at this time he went butterfly hunting, the symbolism of which is apt; specimens were deposited with museums and universities, and a volume of his papers on the subject has been published.

Efficiency

Switzerland and Japan are both Fives (see appendix No. 5). They are the two countries whose efficiency is proverbial: where 'the trains always run on time.' The efficient Five is industrious, regulated, precise, and even-tempered; he thinks ahead in plan and contingency. It will be observed that most of these are also traits of the One who feels under an obligation to do things right and escape censure. In the Five, efficiency promotes a sense of neutral wellbeing, less due to achievement than to what he insulates himself from – all that he does not have to put up with – by way of the unscheduled (i.e. unregulated) making plans go awry and, in business, the queries, requests, and complaints stemming from work that could have been done better. Insulation is a state peculiar to the Five and recurs throughout this chapter. He further compartmentalizes the various sectors of his life, so that one does not wash over into another, and each can be handled 'cleanly'.

Given the choice, he may prefer to deal with matters via the internet, letter etc., so that they are set out before him and can be pondered over in peace and quiet. In a face-to-face encounter time may be spent in aimless conversation, which is pleasant enough for a Two or a Nine who fancies a chat, but merely annoying and distracting to him; or subjects could be raised for which he is unprepared ('Forewarned is forearmed'). Brevity of manner or a crisp tone on his part should not be assumed to be coldness.

Moderation

Calmness and detachment are traits of the moderate Five. He knows that thinking is clouded by emotion; that to focus on the instant alone distorts judgment and may excite by its proximity; and that in enthusiasm points can be overlooked.

It should not be inferred from the foregoing that the Five does not have emotions. Especially in 5-4, they can be experienced inwardly in their own time more than they are expressed.

Professions are gravitated to where quiet is the norm. Apart from academic fields they include medicine, the laboratory technician (one of the classes of technician referred to in the tabulation under 'Cast of mind' above), optician, undertaker, or pathologist. He could also be the mountaineer, long-distance runner, or lone traveller. This stereotype should not be allowed to obscure the fact that many Fives have jobs with a public face, e.g. as journalist or accountant.

Like love, calm radiates. The dentist who is welcoming, calm, skilled in techniques that lessen pain and who, while not glossing over the work to be done on his patient, does not make a 'big deal' of it, transmits some of that calm to the patient and has his trust and cooperation accordingly.

If he is inclined to study and contemplation the type is often attracted to religion. "Be still, and know that I am God" (Psalms 46:10) is an injunction especially addressed to him. The vocation is suited to 5-4 in its mysticism, and to 5-6 in its commitment to belief. A monastic lifestyle combines religious observance, peace, regulation, and contemplation. Serenity in the Five is the resilience of the Seven toned down; is this the quality which in theosophy is termed 'divine indifference'?

In 5-4, stillness of mind can take more exotic forms such as telepathy, clairvoyance, or remote viewing – this last a literal example of psychic far-sightedness. Psychism in general is a broader category (e.g. the Two, Five, or Seven).

Fundamental freedoms

The satellite television station Al-Jazeera broadcasts from Doha, the capital of Qatar, which is 5-4. The station began operation in 1996, and has thrived in the unfettered press environment which emerged after the present Emir deposed his father in a bloodless coup in 1995. Censorship of the media was revoked in 1996.

During the campaign against terrorism in Afghanistan in the autumn of 2001, Al-Jazeera was the only station with a live link to Kabul, and the exclusive news source to the outside world of footage of the enclaved Taliban regime.

When the first of the infamous and taunting video recordings by Osama bin Laden was delivered to the station it was put on the air forthwith and watched with fascination worldwide, having been unseen by Al-Jazeera's executives but with their permission. As one said later, "We trust our reporters." (bin Laden is a 3-4 whose psychological motivation would seem to be a sense of humiliation: when Iraq invaded Kuwait in 1990, Saudi Arabia rejected his offer of 30,000 Afghan veterans for its defence, instead accepting U.S. troops. In a propaganda ('training') video, bin Laden makes the statement: "The entire Muslim world is being humiliated.")

In what was, from the Five standpoint of freedom of speech, a turn of events comical for its irony, the BBC had formerly set up an Arabic-language television channel and contracted with a Saudi Arabian satellite company to broadcast the programmes. Before long the Saudi component of the venture withdrew, objecting to the content. The Emir of Qatar offered to fund an independent station – AlJazeera -which was duly joined by BBC-trained staff.

A biased view is one that is held irrespective of the facts, and is undermined by the freedoms of speech and information, the means of bringing them about being communication and assembly. A reasoned view presupposes exposure to what lies on either side of the balance.

Freedom of thought – hence of expression – is vitiated by being subjected to influences which seek not to inform, but to dictate how the individual is to think and act (see 'Influence and control' in chapter Five).

Pragmatism

This doctrine was once alternatively known as practicalism. To the pragmatist, the meaning of an idea – hence its value – resides in its practical consequences.

Pragmatism is a blend of foresight, moderation, and accommodation. The trait is incompatible with fixed attitudes or the ideal, neither of which heeds consequences, as such relating more to 5-6 than to 5-4; and with the rash action, the consequences of which can not be foreseen or are gambled on. To those who are not in the know, the pragmatist may seem to be changeable in his direction or – in biding his time – lacking in resolve. Pragmatism is not to be confused with expediency (e.g. by the Three), which is the use of a device to facilitate the desired result.

An example of the pragmatist as statesman is Ho Chi Minh (see appendix No.4). With colleagues, he founded the Indochinese Communist Party in 1930, yet his mentors in Moscow had periodic cause to wonder whether his allegiance was to Communism or to Vietnam. In fact, his strategy moulded Communism to conditions in Vietnam, and had to accommodate itself to the ideological rift in the 1950s between the Soviet Union and China, from both of which he managed to extract aid.

Reform (5-6)

As a name for the One, the Reformer was discussed in chapter three. The average One lives 'by the book'; he tries to conform to the best of the moral and legal code as it exists, not to change it. If he is a reformer, he works towards a more ordered society in which 'things mean what they say', and compliance with duty and obligation is made clear. In reform of the law or religious practice, his goal is to eradicate laxity, obscurantism, and the finely argued over, and to restore the straightforward. Thomas Cranmer (1-9) is an example of a religious reformer.

The Three is the type to entertain ideas of reform as a 'grand project', as in organizational reform of the health service or social security (see 'Orientation by result' in chapter five). Thoroughgoing reform, however, calls for devotion and patience on a scale which the Three can seldom match; still less in altruism, where the purpose is social betterment.

In terms of the ethos of the Five, his motivation in instituting reform is either to promote, or raise standards of, education and learning; or to awaken the social conscience with the light of knowledge.

William Tyndale was martyred in 1536. He believed that the Bible alone should determine ecclesiastical procedure and intended that, by the homely language of his translation with its Anglo-Saxon words and spoken idioms, even "a boy that driveth the plough" would be enabled to read the Bible with understanding. He worked from the original (i.e. 'pure': the Five) Hebrew and Greek texts, and his translation was the prime basis for the Authorized Version of 1611. To him we owe the beauty, simple and sublime, of passages like "for in him we live, and move, and have our being" (Acts 17:28). His last words are recorded as "Lord! Open the King of England's eyes."

Elizabeth Fry was a minister and speaker in the Society of Friends who in the early 1800s set herself to improving the conditions of women prisoners in Newgate, providing them with decent clothing, starting a school, and expounding the Bible. She visited prisons around the country, founded prison visiting societies, and exposed the misery of convicts on the ships in which they were transported overseas.

In the Victorian era, the Earl of Shaftesbury presided over the reform of conditions in factories and coal mines, the provision of low-cost housing, and the 'ragged schools' at which destitute children were educated free. He secured legislation whereby the insane would no longer be treated as social outcasts. In his later years he was much consulted on issues of social and religious controversy. His ethical sense can not be distinguished from that of the One.

As a curious exception to this classification by type, Thomas Barnardo (see appendix No.4) is a Seven, but does have components of the Five and the Six.

Self-sufficiency

A gregarious person lets others come and go in his social space, as he does in theirs. The self-sufficient Five controls his space, and can react adversely to its being entered without his consent.

As a Five, his needs are knowledge-based more than they are material. Knowledge being a free resource, the satisfaction of those needs does not normally have to impinge on the social life of anyone else.

For recreation, he has a few friends with whom he discusses ideas, or plays games of strategy. As an academic he may attend or speak at lectures, which for him are a social occasion and study session in one.

It has to be said that the Five does not have a good record in relationships (the Nine may have the best), having a low emotional responsiveness, and in a relationship he has to relax control of his space. (What does make for a lasting partnership is a sense of newfound rootedness, for the Five who felt before that he did not belong anywhere; this is not to be confused with the sense of belonging in the Six.)

Symptoms of control of a kind that is alarmingly rigid are a cause for psychiatric intervention, e.g. the youngster who lives almost as a recluse in the family, and only consents to answering a specified and tiny number of questions from a worried parent, after which 'time is up'; or the compulsive list-maker, for whom every last thing must be inventoried. Control in the Five is self-insulating, and the reverse of control by prevailing over (the Eight).

When the Five overly abstracts himself in the mind, he fails in the down-to-earth. What he says or does causes surprise, or his relationships are disordered or naive. In overtaxing his mentality he can become schizotypal and, in a grandiose but introverted way, deluded (see 'Misconceptions as to type' below).

If he should venture into a worldly arena that is not firmly within his competence, his approach is skewed. Some of his thoughts miss the mark, have to be fathomed for their meaning, or are misinterpreted. His attitudes may seem contradictory (e.g. both tolerant and intolerant), though he would defend himself against the charge.

Social deficit

Interested as he is in facts, ideas, and theories, the Five who lives in the mind can be unsure of how to behave in company so as not to feel like an alien presence who is engulfed and would dearly wish to be somewhere else. (6-5 can react not by feeling engulfed but that he stands out, and does know how to behave).

In a formal gathering he may be seen on occasion taking his cue from others, or glancing around for confirmation that he is not out of step. His anxiety is eased if the agenda is not departed from, so that there are no surprises.

If he has a 'take it or leave it' attitude, he can be tactless, peremptory, or high-handed. To the charge of being tactless, he would retort that communication serves to convey facts, and is not a conduit for being considerate. His sense of humour is either dry or of a robustness that can offend.

Having said or done what he intended, he can be peremptory in not wanting to engage in debate over it. Among his reasons could be a lack of time or enthusiasm, or that an emotional issue is at stake.

In being high-handed, he arrives by his own reasoning at a resolution of what ought to be decided by discussion, or what is not for him to decide. By his logic this is a measure of efficiency and economy, as conversational meander is done away with. Others are vexed by his semi-detachment, and antagonized by his disrespect in making and acting on decisions without their say.

He does not know how to deal with his own displeasure, which if it should mutate into resentment is the equivalent of a time-bomb.

A company director who is a Five smothered his wife to death after she had nagged him, when he brought her the morning papers, over the purchase of a flat which he judged to be too expensive for them, and accused him of being mean. He stated in court, "It was so grossly unfair, so hurtful because I give so much of my time to worthy causes, but then, somehow I put my hands on my wife. It was the first time I had ever done this in anger I have no idea of what I meant to do." Being an efficient and compartmentalizing Five, after tidying the bedroom he had planned his work schedule for the day, during which he clinched a £1 million takeover deal and paid £15,000 in bills. He gave himself up at five o'clock, confessing to what he had done. An employee of the company of which he had once been chief executive thought that "He was someone you never questioned. If he wanted something done, then you just did it."

Fastidiousness

In the Five, fastidiousness has to do not with refinement but mostly with a wish to avoid physical contact. Examples are the lad in the playground who declines the cigarette that is passed around, as other mouths have tasted it – and contaminated it; or the man who inadvertently brushes against a woman, and can not wait to apologize, the subtext being: "I should not have touched you." The Five who fears showing himself up is fastidious in self-control.

Since there is no sexual relationship without contact, the person who is physically fastidious and sexually needy has to satisfy himself with fantasy and the inanimate. The Five is the largest consumer of pornography, a voyeur (the Seven is another), and a solitary devotee of the fetish. Pornographic magazines and videos featuring the under-age can be routinely bought in Japan (a Five), which Interpol estimates accounts for 80% of commercial child pornography on the internet. (The Five who is a paedophile – and not fastidious

– comes into contact with youngsters via teaching, the priesthood, youth work/training, at swimming pools, and since recent times on the internet. The Seven is another type to be considered in diagnosis.)

It may be speculated that a percentage of anorexia – as 'contamination by the intake of food' – originates with this trait (5-4 more than 5-6?), which would also be an unarguable, if self-defeating, demonstration of the anorexic's control of his or her space, and is to be distinguished from the emotionally controlling Two who has disintegrated to the Eight; likewise delusions of exalted purity that have a religious overtone.

Bodily invasiveness (the Five) is a theme of the controversial (the Six) film director David Cronenberg, who is 6-7 with an admixture of the Five.

Lack of connection to life

To be adrift in the mind, with nothing in view that would impel with purpose along any one route, spells emptiness of being. The Five in this state goes through the motions of living, seeing to his instinctual needs but otherwise bereft of stimuli. He favours employment out of doors, either in peace by himself, or in impersonal surroundings where he is not disadvantaged in being untalkative. He could be a casual labourer, gardener, or goods vehicle delivery man. In a literal sense and not to disparage him, 5-6 can be the most nondescript subtype on the Enneagram.

A pathological lack of connection can manifest itself in schizoid personality disorder, which is characterized by unresponsiveness and emotional non-attachment; and in strange habits such as prolonged staring, laughing for no reason, or chanting to himself. Whilst rare, acts that are perverse and motiveless may be committed.

If he is both disconnected and frustrated by existing, he blanks out the everyday and invents in his imagination a dark and deviant world of his own, which may be nihilist, pornographic, necrophiliac, or satanist, and in which his emotional emptiness – i.e. coldness – is a factor. His darkness is the underside of the enlightenment of the healthy Five.

An amusing example of someone who is intelligent but devoid of imagination, and whose disconnection is therefore not total, is David England, who is 5-6. News of what he had done was headlined in one paper: "Tedious career of master fraudster ends in prison." The odd headline was accurate, for "So staggeringly boring was his life that its details will forever overshadow his work. The proceeds of one of Britain's biggest bank scams funded underwear, herbal teabags, vegan food, stamps and taxis." Over three years he created nine identities and set up some 90 bank accounts, defrauding a dozen banks out of £777,000. His 12-hour working days were spent moving money around: withdrawing, paying in, and applying for loans. He would pose as an accountant or geologist – either could be a profession of his subtype–, and was compared to a 'champion plate spinner.' The only lavish item that he bought was a Rolex watch; he did not drink, smoke, or gamble. The bulk of his outgoings went on rent and service charges on the properties that were a front for his identities. A filing cabinet containing many dozens of identity files, and 200 bank and credit cards, was the nub of his operation. He had ten driving licences, nine of them in false names – yet he did not own a car! He was about to flee the country but would presumably not have desisted from his practice, since his mental horizon stretched no further.

Escapism

On its face, this trait can not be distinguished from escapism in the Seven: the motivation is the same; but the mechanism is not. The Five escapes from what can not be endured not by disguise, e.g. the performer who hides behind his act or the homosexual who marries, but by putting distance between himself and that from which he is in flight. He may have a sense as of being pursued. As one wrote, "It's like playing a game of tag and I'm it." Or as a remorseful Five admitted in court, "I've been running from first one thing and then another all my life. There are some things that you just can't run from, and this being one of those." A likely cause of the desire to escape – which can be into drugs and crime – is an abusive parent. The escape route of last resort is suicide.

Hypersensitivity

The Five wishes to be accepted for who he is without disparagement or close examination. If he is hypersensitive, he reacts with an unexternalized intensity to being shown up: made fun of, picked on, or as the object of rumour that there is something not normal about him. When his control gives way, the sentiment objectifies itself as a rage against those whom he holds to blame. By nature he is reserved or shy, but not apathetic; a schizoid Five could not be hypersensitive.

David Copeland is 5-4. In 1999 he conducted a nail-bombing campaign at three sites in London which left three dead and 139 injured. At the age of thirteen he had been treated for his small size and delayed adolescence, which he found very humiliating, and alleged that since then his family had taunted him about his sexuality. The third bomb targeted a gay pub. He is by no means unusual in this category for his mindset of hate, and his obsession with guns or bombs, Nazi regalia, and heavy metal music. (Music played at loudest volume blanks out the world; see 'Lack of connection to life' above).

Thomas Hamilton, a Five who in 1996 shot dead 16 children and their teacher in Dunblane, could be considered peripheral to this category.

Paranoia (5-6)

Traits of the paranoid 5-6 are a sense of grievance and persecution, contempt, and suspiciousness. His grievances are about what he claims either to have been subjected to, or to be rightly his but denied to him. They are voiced more to third parties than direct to those concerned – who could refute them. In writing, he can be intellectually pretentious and verbose. If he is unable to move on from a grievance he may conduct a vendetta, and should not be mistaken for the unforgiving Eight. By way of comparison, traits of the paranoid 6-5 are social withdrawal, lack of trust, and a state of defendedness that is fed by incessant and manufactured suspicions.

In a letter of January 2000, Ian Brady informed the BBC that "As you are aware, I have studied logic, the science of argument, the application of convoluted dialectics and rationale to personal deposition and evidential factors." He has complained that in Ashworth high-security hospital "I am buried in subnormals", and in recent years believes that the Home Office is intent on poisoning him.

To comment on the symptoms of paranoia in the World Health Organization classification, what correlates with an undue sensitivity to setbacks is fatalism, e.g. in the Six, not a sense of grievance. To be unforgiving assumes that there is something to forgive; the grievances of the paranoid Five are always overdone, if not imaginary. Suspicions over where a partner's affections lie relate to the possessiveness of the insecure Six, where the core issue is a lack of trust. Conspiracy theories that are not of self-reference are thought up by the Five (5-4), and grandly rationalized with his 'select' knowledge of the arcane.

Image fixation

A traumatic or arresting incident can so impress itself on the psyche of the Five that, whether he was a participant or an onlooker, he is driven by a compulsion to reenact it. The incident could be said to be fetishized. With the exception of Dennis Nilsen (see appendix No.4: the Six), the examples that I have are 5-6. A variant of the trait is a fixation on a living person (e.g. as an emotional transference) who for the Five is intimately associated therewith.

Harold Shipman is now thought to have killed more than two hundred of his patients. When he was seventeen, he had watched as his mother died a slow and painful death from cancer. Many of his victims died not in bed but sitting in a chair, as his mother had been when morphine was administered to her.

Jeffrey Dahmer killed 17 young men, preserving body parts for an intended 'shrine'. At the age of four he had been operated on for a hernia; what was being done was not explained to him, and he evidently felt pain and fear. The episode would seem to have translated itself into a fixation on the bodily invasive, and most of all on the intestines. Dahmer was very markedly schizoid.

A youth worker in southern Russia witnessed a car accident in which a boy in school uniform died. He saw flames and smelt petrol, and had dreams about the accident which sexually aroused him. To relive what he had seen, he procured boys wearing the uniform; in particular the black shoes were a fetish for him. He killed seven, setting the remains on fire with petrol. So tightly sealed from each other were the compartments of his mind that under interrogation he spoke freely of his background and what he had done, yet revealed himself to be aghast at the idea of doing his job other than sober.

Miscellaneous traits

It is likely that the Five is prominent in sports where precision and calmness are essential, e.g. snooker, darts, golf, archery

Minimalism in design, art, performance: efficiency with

economy

Intellectual superiority: disdain, conceit

Petty; officious: 'rules are rules', where the emphasis is not
on what is right and reasonable (the One), but on what
is prescribed

Professional envy (5-6)

Phobias related to physical contact

Misconceptions as to type

The Five's world is not a dangerous place: that is a perception
of the Six; but he may have to be in control of his space for
anxiety not to arise.

The power broker is a name given to the Eight who is
deal-driven and has accumulated great wealth. Some of the
most powerful dealmakers are, however, not Eights but Fives.
The businesses which are to figure in a deal are, so to speak,
laid out on the chess board that is the mind of the Five, who
assesses ahead of the competition the permutations that are
indicated. His deals can be a web of complexity, and details of
them precise yet impenetrable.

Frustration that is vented with force on an inanimate
object in solitude is more a trait of the Five than of the One.
An example is someone who lived by woodlands and would
be heard 'attacking' a tree trunk with an axe. Another outlet
would be to vandalize a derelict building.

Chapter 8

TYPE SIX: COMMITMENT/SECURITY

Orientation: Towards

Outsider state: Separated. Abandoned: need for something to adhere to

Primary resonance: TYPE ONE

Secondary resonance: TYPE FOUR

6-5:   A position is taken, and upheld or defended, that is distinct from, more than relative. In commitment, a tendency to self-reliance

6-7:   A position is taken, and upheld or defended, that is relative (e.g. one of many). In commitment, a tendency to mutual reliance

Comment on name of type

It may be wondered how the names given to the Six – the Loyalist, the Devil's Advocate, and the Questioner – can define one and the same type, since on their face they have no connection. That said, the first two names do describe categories of the Six, though not the type overall.

Commitment can mean loyalty, in belonging to and identifying with. When loyalty is subjected to pressure, the bond between the Six and the object of his loyalty is hardened, weakened, or broken. If hardened, and devoted to a worthy cause, the trait may be indistinguishable from the faith of the

One, except for its communal or group dimension.

Disloyalty is as much a feature of the Six as is loyalty. An encyclopaedic source calls King Charles I, who is 6-5 (see appendix No.4), "an irresolute enemy and a false friend"; as a captive, he made a secret treaty with the Scots. What of his loyalty to the institution of which he was the embodiment? At its birth the United States was 6-7 (see same appendix); the event having come about by rebellion, loyalties were divided.

The ramifications of loyalty may be illustrated with a hypothetical example. A gang member who is a Six is being loyal to his mates in having nothing to say when questioned about a misdeed for which he knows one of them to be responsible. His motive(s) could be any of these: the desire not to forgo his sense of belonging; the respect of his peers: he must give no hint of wavering in his loyalty; the psychological security of strength in numbers; an attitude of 'better the devil you know'; or the averting of threat to his safety from them. If his conscience is stronger than these considerations, he could be disloyal to the gang by making a stand, in speaking out and taking his chances as to reprisal.

Loyalty should not be assumed to relate to the Six unless motivated by commitment or security. Loyalty as an ethical duty suggests the One; out of obedience, the One or the Six; due to emotional dependence, the Two or the Six; to preserve a favourable image, the Three; and with the force of an oath, the Eight.

In its everyday connotation, devil's advocate is a negative term (in which respect, why would anyone wish to assign it to himself?) which does not remotely measure up to the substance of the Six, reducing it in parody merely to a habit of contrariness. Indeed there are Sixes who are argumentative; they do so to defend their views or position, to draw out the views of others, to test for reaction to their own, to ascertain who is on the side of whom, or to be noticed. They are exemplified by the journalist or radio host charged with

116

generating heated debate by airing absurdly overstated views in order to stimulate sales or audience figures; a performance legitimized by the label 'controversial'. Modern art is an area where the creative and the controversial are intermixed. The Five (5-6) can also be argumentative, over the truth of an issue.

From the Roman Catholic ritual for canonization, the original meaning of acting as devil's advocate is to probe for defect in the sterling character of the one proposed, in a setting that places him on trial, and to ensure that the rules of law are observed. This is a role of the One, not the Six.

To question is not a trait of the Six alone, but of the triad of the Four, Five, and Six (see tabulation No.4 in appendix No.l). The Four questions as an immigrant would, in forming his appreciations of living in a foreign land; the Five, for meaning and understanding; and the Six, to test for trust-worthiness and safety.

Outsider state

Characteristics of abandonment in real life are detailed in chapter four, in examining the outsider state of the Two ('unwanted') in its resemblance to that of the Six.

In the outsider state, the Six was abandoned because his sense of belonging or likeability was not strong enough. He has to reattach himself to some aspect of his environment, and does so with a hold that can be tenacious. In its persistence, tenacity should not be mistaken for resilience (the Seven). At the extreme the tenacious person is the fanatic.

The risk or fear of abandonment can be negated altogether not by a relationship – the durability of which is not guaranteed – but by attachment to a group that stands for, and defends, a set of shared social values (see heading below).

He has those traits that make for agreeable company and constructive association. He is likeable, gregarious, obliging, responsible, conscientious, loyal, and society-orientated (as an extension of belonging), and he does not make decisions that impact on others without discussion with them. In short, he is well regarded and actively engaged. This is not the contrivance of an impression: he is not selling himself on promise. He can have the same problem as the Two in turning down requests for help, his motive being anxiety over being thought to be – or behind his back spoken of as being – less than whole-heartedly committed ("I was counting on you." "Is he with us or what?").

Psychological symptoms of a sense of abandonment are a craving to belong; and a craving to be liked or for affection (shared with the emotionally needy Two). The latter can be a cause of promiscuity.

Commitment

It has been stated that the faith of the One has more of attitude than of action, and stands firm in adversity. In the Six, faith has as much of action as of attitude, and goes forward in adversity.

The Apostle Paul is a Six. By argument and exhortation, he sought to persuade his audience of the truth of his teachings. He had studied law; the Six is the lawyer for whom there are necessarily two sides to every issue: for and against; he may be on either. Paul experienced both sides; before his conversion he had zealously persecuted the Christians, who were seen as a threat to the Pharisees, and as an apostle he was himself constantly persecuted.

Commitment in general has to do with those occupations which bind society together and regulate its wellbeing. Foremost among them are the defence of the nation, the practice of law, crime prevention and detection, the prison service, education, healthcare, and welfare. The interdependence of the profession and society at large is evident in some of these areas. In the armed forces, imperatives converge: the eyes and ears of one man could save the day for a colleague or the unit; or conversely, safety could be endangered by one underperformer.

Causes of injustice are promoted by the Six, through the rousing and rallying of the like-minded ("We all feel the same"), and strength of numbers. From the beginning he is taken notice of – an essential for any campaign if it is to succeed –, due to the demonstrativeness of his methods, his demands for a hearing, and the one-sidedness of his arguments.

To dispel any ambiguity in relation to this heading, it should be understood that commitment can also be the driving force in the Five whose motivation is not the persuasive truth of belief, as for the Six, but enlightenment by the facts. His enemy is not the antagonist to his belief, but the closed mind. Two examples who are 5-6 are Alfred Kinsey and John Pilger.

Trade unions are bodies to which the Six is responsive. Their cause is the betterment of workers' conditions, fairness of pay, and the righting of wrongs. They foster fraternalism of labour.

In the U.K., an issue of conscience arises for teachers and doctors which some who are Ones or Sixes would feel acutely: how to square conscientious care with the obligations of a bureaucratic workload decreed by a result-orientated administration.

When a business which for decades has been the backbone in the life of a town is to close down, it is the Six who is in the vanguard of protest against the decision, insisting on discussions with management, and (with the Two) doing what he can to combat defeatism and to rally support for the struggle.

Security

For the Six, security comprises an upbringing in a loving and stable family, trust, and self-assurance. Unless he makes his own stand as an individualist or rebel, he is sure of his ground (trust) and capabilities (self-assurance), and the dependability of his intimates is proven. Habits, attitudes, and beliefs are held to; they are not much questioned or changed.

The industrious Six does not stop at a passable knowledge of his chosen field but progresses to a thorough grasp, so that he can be seen to have done a good job, and is protected somewhat from mistakes, i.e. from being shown up or disapproved of.

As a conformist, he is aware of the risks in overreaching himself. His preference is not for self-employment; he is comfortable with a format prescribed by line of authority and the rule-book.

Recognition is, of course, a source of security to the Six as performer – as it is to the Seven with a Six subtype. In this role, if he plays up to the image expected of him he has security of response from his audience, but may be stuck with the stereotype. If he should be drawn to branching out, he has to weigh the loss of security against his onward development.

An undeserved security accrues to professions which regulate themselves, since they are cushioned from meaningful accountability, and close ranks if under threat. The polarized 'us and them' attitude, endemic in such institutions, resents attack on their closeted world. Cover-ups mostly result either from the foregoing, or from a Three who has to preserve his image from being tarnished.

If his parental identity is not fully known or confused, as a youngster he may feel that he does not have a family to belong to. Actual examples of such Sixes are a woman who, until told of her parentage at the age of twelve, thought that her grandfather was her father; and a man who was given up for adoption at birth because his mother, pregnant with him and abandoned by her husband- who was not the father –, was told by her partner to "get rid of' the child. Twenty years later, the man in this last example searched through records and did make contact with his real mother, but by then the link was not to last.

The contemporary

This heading yields an insight into the quality of a type when contrasted with that of its secondary resonance, which for the Six is the Four. To the Six, life is lived in present time; to the Four, it is timeless. Fashion ('Here today and gone tomorrow'), graphic design, and modern art are creations of the Six, with input from the Seven.

The artist as Six has a sense of form and of a desired effect. He may wander far from the orthodoxy of the canvas, into construction or agglomeration. In contradistinction to the aesthetic (the Four), his art can be in bad taste or depict aberration, decay, or wreckage. It has been said that art redeems the exiled soul – a sentiment of the Four with which the Six would have no patience.

Photography is an art form of the Six, in so far as the objective is to capture a live moment that will not repeat itself.

Conflict of impulses

Princess Margaret is 6-7. By the 1950s she had begun a romance with a married man in the royal household, Peter Townsend; he divorced his wife in 1952. In 1953, when she was 23, they informed her sister, Queen Elizabeth, of their wish to marry. The Queen is head of the Church of England, which forbad divorce, and under the Royal Marriages Act she would have had to consent to the marriage if Margaret were under 25; after that age, she could marry with the consent of Parliament. A Cabinet session resolved that the marriage could not be approved, and it was unlikely that this position would soften when she turned 25. Margaret could not look for advice to the Queen, who was of the view that she should be free to reach her own decision. In 1955 she was told that if she proceeded she would be deprived of her rights, privileges, and income, and would have to be married abroad and not return to the U.K. for some years. Later that year she renounced the idea.

This is an example of desires versus obligation or conscience: what someone wants to do versus what he ought to do. The predicament of Margaret is not without mixed motives on account of the subsidiary dilemmas of love for the partner versus abandonment by the family (emotional), and love for the partner versus loss of security (material).

The same state of desires versus conscience would assail a Six who could not dismiss from his mind a wrong that he had done to someone else for which he had not yet been found out, his desires urging him to play safe and say nothing, while his conscience urged him to come clean.

Another manifestation is to be oneself versus conformity. A gang member as a new entrant may want to prove himself, so earning the gang's friendship and respect; but their activities are ones about which he is uneasy, either because he doubts that he has the ability (i.e. he will be shown up), or from a standpoint of conscience (i.e. they are wrong) or of danger. The trait is one of the Six or the Seven (7-6), motivated by the desire to be the equal of, or better than, one's peers.

A clash in belonging is represented by the traditional versus the contemporary. The Six who emigrates to the West from a country where the authority of tradition rules may be torn between abandoning his inherited identity and pleas from his family ("You belong with us"), and being accepted by conforming to his new surroundings. If he forms a cross-cultural relationship, it is not only his identity but also his personal loyalties that are tested, which could give him even more of a bad conscience.

Lack of trust

Relationships are the area of life in which trust is endlessly problematical for the insecure Six. He would like always to know where his partner is, what she is doing, and with whom. If she should come home late from an outing, his greeting to her is not "How did it go, darling?", but a sarcastic and semi-accusing "So you're back, then." His 'welcome' does not strike her as worth acknowledging, so he probably never learns the reason for her lateness, having sabotaged his own attempt at finding out. Brooding over the episode only increases his insecurity, and distance between them is created by not communicating.

It is ironic that the Six frequently teams up with the Seven who, casting her in the above role, is not renowned for keeping to a timetable – still less for bothering with the worst-case suspicions that the Six will have thought up; nor are matters improved if she makes light of it, which would frustrate him and be interpreted as an evasion ("What does she have to hide?").

When the Six for whom lack of trust runs deep – who believes that life would never deal him a winning hand – is presented with an opportunity that seems too good to be true, far from embracing it with open arms, he has to validate his negative perception by discovering flaws.

A sentiment that can disguise lack of trust is scorn. A woman who is a Six, having witnessed the marital inharmony of her parents, felt that men are "both comic and a menace", and made fun of her sister's boyfriends. Envy could also figure in such a case.

The mistrusting Six whose aims are aggressive veils them and moves step by step, verifying at each stage that the gain is safe. This was Hitler's approach throughout the 1930s, notably in reoccupying the Rhineland in March 1936, over which he admitted that if the French had marched in, "We would have had to withdraw with our tails between our legs." To reassure Europe, every fear that he aroused he would assuage with renewed talk of peace and cooperation, portraying himself as the apostle of order and the enemy as Bolshevist chaos. The imagery is that of a cautious gambler, and of bets that pay off and stakes raised.

Lack of confidence

Harry Truman is remembered as a straight-dealing man who placed the defence (the Six) of the United States on its postwar footing; he is 6-7. He was also unprepared to take office as President, ignorant of the major issues, and quite devoid of confidence. He did however realize that he had to appear confident, which in an executive capacity means being decisively in command. At a conference on the Polish question (the composition of its government to accord with Soviet interests) in April 1945, the Soviet Foreign Minister, V.M.Molotov, protested that "I have never been talked to like that in my life", to which Truman retorted, "Carry out your agreements and you won't get talked to like that." Yet days later Truman asked his aides, "I want to know what you think. Did I do right?"

Truman's aggressive stance in conversation with Molotov was a psychological compensation for his insecurity. In theory, the strategy for a Six in negotiation should be to hold his fire and to draw out the thinking of the other party so that doubts, suspicions, and false assumptions are clarified, and he can gauge what latitude might exist for the fair bargaining of demand and concession.

On 21st July 1945, the sixth day of the Potsdam Conference, the document reporting in detail on the successful test detonation of the atomic bomb was received by the American delegation. This was the outcome on which Truman had gambled when scheduling the dates of the conference. On his performance at the afternoon session that same day Churchill commented, as recorded by the

American Secretary of War Henry L. Stimson, that "When he got to the meeting after having read this report he was a changed man. He told the Russians just where they got on and off and generally bossed the whole meeting." Truman confirmed to Stimson the impact of the bomb on his attitude.

Stalin perceived threat in the brief mention to him on 24th July of a new weapon, and that evening gave orders for Soviet atomic energy research to be accelerated.

Negative attitude to authority

Authority is not challenged by the healthy Six, except incidentally in commitment to a cause.

The main reasons for a negative attitude – sullen, rebellious, aggressive – to authority are parental neglect or incompetence (absence of a sense of belonging, sound behavioural guidelines, or boundaries); the exercising of parental authority not as a standard and with decency, but inconsistently or excessively (a switch in the tenor of authority from original to substitute parent would be relevant); the youngster falls in with bad company (parental neglect could be a factor); his parents do not respect each other; he is picked on by his peers and made to feel an outsider (one reason for the 'outlaw' mentality); he is not allowed his self-respect, or it is worn down by attack ("You are worthless" – a theme about which the management and warders of every prison and boot camp would do well to educate themselves if their system is ever to work); or he does not have a permanent home. The presence of respect in two of these categories should be noted: to transgress is to cross a boundary prescribed by authority; to disrespect is to cross someone else's boundary. In attitude, the Six learns from family and the social scene. If he is not respected, or sees scant respect around him, why should he have respect?

On the street, that segment of youth which wears its demand for respect like insignia and postures threateningly is a feature of the type.

Misunderstandings abound concerning this trait. It is said that the Six has on occasion to assert himself by reacting against authority, lest he be not respected for over-conformity. Why would a conformist Six put at risk his sense of belonging by antagonizing his security source on a whim? His self-respect is in any event not a function of conformity or non-conformity, but of worth; and any action of his that repercusses on others – a security source might not be his alone – diminishes that worth.

His distrust – if he has it – is of the world at large, and only of authority when linked with a perception of suspect personal intent.

Distrust of corporate authority, where not accessible or transparent, is a trait of the Five ("Do we know what is going on in there?" "Why won't they divulge the information?").

To submit, not to rebel, is the normal response to oppression, together with a degree of fatalism; the Soviet Union was 6-7. It is typically the Seven, with his life-affirming resilience, who rebels against oppression.

Self-contradiction

If the trust of the Six is not abused (e.g. by broken promises), his sense of respect is intact, and he is not under stress (see heading below), all is well. Otherwise he may veer from open to guarded, from candid to evasive, from amenable to stubborn, from equable to overreacting, and so on.

A woman who is a Six regarded marriage as a burden of disrespect which turns women into 'downtrodden housewives'. She sought 'lofty' relationships, yet did not at all wish to be childless; on first being proposed to, she was depressed. This sounds like a Four whose sights are set on an unsatisfiable ideal, but is not; her jaundiced outlook was formed entirely in life. She later had numerous boyfriends who were unfaithful and whom she mistreated.

Prejudice

Nowhere is the contrast between the Six and the Four more marked than in the matter of prejudice. To the Four, differences of orientation (e.g. in religion, sexuality), colour, or custom are a cultural enrichment – against which the prejudice of an unhealthy Six is a defence. He associates with those who have the same sentiments, and does not inform himself about the target of his prejudice; enlightenment would weaken his stand. His fear can be tinged with envy, or projected as hatred if he has disintegrated to the Three.

Stress

Factors which conspire to induce stress in the Six are anxiety over his performance – at home or at work – being up to par, or not letting the side down ("What will they think of me if they see that I'm struggling?" "What if I have to ask for assistance?"), as in a job that is too demanding, not least if providing the only source of family income, or if he is self-employed; over-commitment: again, the desire not to let the side down ("It's expected of me"); or a chain of adverse events from which by its cumulative effect he arrives at the despairing notion that he has no way out.

The venting of his frustrations in unaccustomed moodiness in the safety of the home or among close friends is a warning sign; uncommunicativeness, or keeping his distance, is another. When an insecure Six responds to a kindly enquiry with a bad-tempered "I don't need anyone's help" he almost certainly does- but he is not about to 'demean' himself by asking for it.

It may be speculated that a neurotic carefulness in performing a service, as in checking and rechecking the content of something before it goes forward (e.g. a doctor's prescription, or a sum of money) could be a trait of the stressed 6-5, or a Five with a heavy Six subtype.

In 2000 the personal assistant of a member of Parliament

was killed with a sword by a man who is 6-5, during a meeting with constituents. The man had been in contact with his member of Parliament dozens of times over the downturn in his fortunes. He had bought a house with a mortgage secured on his pension rights which he had transferred to his bank from a former employer. The business which he had hoped to establish did not materialize. The house was to have been used as his business premises and was repossessed after he fell in arrears with mortgage repayments – and was allegedly resold for about £100,000 more than he paid for it. He separated from his wife; his sister died; he had two accidents for which he was hospitalized. He was adjudged not to qualify for social security benefit. In his mind everyone was against him (see 'Victim/loser mindset' below).

In the case of suicide, such a state as the above resembles that of a disintegrated Seven.

Schizophrenia

Whilst not in accordance with Enneagram literature, my findings indicate that schizophrenia relates to 6-7, and paranoid schizophrenia to 6-5.

A rationale for the schizophrenic being a Six (6-7) is that he is without psychological defences. His mind is an open space which is randomly invaded, directed, tampered with, listened in to, or emptied. An analogy is a safe (a Six item), in which his thoughts are deposited, withdrawn, jumbled, or had sight of by others of a malign disposition. The authenticity of the thoughts may be argued over (the Six). The safe can be pictured as left open, or as locked, but with parties unknown suspected of having the combination. For his security the schizophrenic has to make what sense he can of the result, hence his misperceptions.

Pete Bullimore is the coordinator of the Hearing Voices Network in his local area; he is 6-7. His first experience of schizophrenia was in 1992, when a social worker arrived at his home to assess the family as foster carers; a voice told him that the visitor was a French spy. Before long, "There was one main demonic voice that started telling me to kill myself, and ten or so in the background that sounded as if a radio had been left on somewhere." In hindsight he thinks that the disorder was triggered by his lifestyle; he had recently begun his own business and was working seven days a week (cf. Michael Abram, below). His life took a turn for the better when he attended a session run by a mental health charity, and his recovery was further hastened when he developed strategies for reducing the effect of the voices, like giving the dominant one "the identity of someone in real life whom I didn't fear."

A man who is 6-7 rose before dawn and ran from his apartment, thinking that the landlord was pursuing him. As he went along, he imagined that voices were speaking to him, and that he "got through the hedge to get into heaven." For a half hour he felt supremely happy. In continuing his walk he spoke to a policeman, who thought that he should be placed in care as he was raving.

In 1999 Michael Abram knifed George Harrison, whom he believed he had been ordered to kill because he was a 'phantom menace'. When Harrison asked him who he was, he replied, "You know who I am." Abram is 6-5. Two months before the attack, as his mother recounted, "We were just chatting when he snapped his fingers and said, 'I've got it – Paul McCartney is a witch but George Harrison is the boss'". He had once had a good job in telesales, but took drugs to relieve the stress. After arguments he broke up with his partner, they had two children. He moved into a dismal flat where he fixated on Oasis; he thought that the song *Wonderwall* was about a wall in his flat. He was fearful of his state, which had been misdiagnosed as being caused by his drug abuse.

Two factors to consider in the antecedents to this incident are the stress that he experienced in his job, and living alone in a 'dismal flat' after having enjoyed a family life (the non-belonging of physical and emotional isolation).

Anthony Joseph is 6-5. In 1998 he killed his social worker, stabbing her more than one hundred times. He believed that she was planning to send him back to hospital to be tortured by fascists. He had a history of carrying knives and not taking his medication – surely because the paranoid element in him suspected that it would do him harm –, and had threatened his mother and hostel staff.

A curious feature in the Six is the commentary and instruction of a persecutory, argumentative, or otherwise negative kind that the person may perceive in his mind towards himself and his actions, whether he is being addressed, or talked about in his presence. In tabulation No.I (see appendix No.I) the Six is defined as being 'at a varying point on the observer/participant spectrum.' The schizophrenic is participant when addressed, and observer when talked about. The Six can be at a fairly central point (with a light Five or Seven subtype), towards the observer end of the spectrum (with a heavier Five subtype), or towards the participant end (with a heavier Seven subtype). The psychological quandary over the schizophrenic is that, his perspective not being stable nor even a product of his consciousness, there can be no idea of where he actually is on the spectrum, technically and in social inclination.

If it is to succeed, treatment has to stabilize the Six psychologically at a determinate point on the observer/participant spectrum, restoring in him a feeling of security in his perceptions.

As a reference source for these and other disorders, the ICD-10 Classification of Mental and Behavioural Disorders of the World Health Organization, Geneva, is recommended. Schizophrenia should not be confused with schizoid personality disorder, which is treated in chapter seven; for paranoia, see 'Miscellaneous traits' below.

Victim/loser mindset

All that the Six who sees no life ahead of him can opt for is the defence mechanism of psychological projection, or suicide. He is profoundly resentful, envious, and self-pitying. He casts around for scapegoats whom he can blame. In a last stand he can be a spree killer (6-5 more than 6-7), and in motivation should be distinguished from the Five who is hypersensitive or pathologically aware of what his inhibited nature has caused him to miss out on (5-4), and the one who has a sense of grievance, which can be combined with envy (5- 6).

If he has always been frustrated by life, he feels that he is a born loser: that he has been let down or betrayed at every tum. He has a sense of fatedness, even of a 'pact with death'.

Hitler, a 6-7, marshalled this negativity of sentiment in the Weimar Republic – which was itself 6-7 – and ever thereafter, and without it would have been a nobody; for far from laying to rest the enmity between Germany and the allied powers, the framers of the Treaty ('Diktat') of Versailles knowingly set about the task of depriving Germany of her self-respect (the Six), breeding the resentment (the Six) that – with the aid of exaggeration and fabrication by the treaty's opponents, and the Great Depression – would be as oxygen to Hitler in steering the nation to catastrophe.

The war guilt clause of the treaty, being an arbitrary and subjective judgment, and to Germany an outrage, converted itself in the nation's psyche into the projection of blame (the Six).

It is unwise to aim for a settlement with a country which is a Six in Germany's post-1918 psychological state with treaty clauses that are protracted over time (e.g. reparations: payments were rescheduled under the Dawes Plan of 1924 and the Young Plan of 1929 – which crystallized opposition to the Weimar 'system'–, and were not resumed after the Lausanne agreement three years later), since the resentment against them and its incitement become semi-permanent, opening the door to ongoing debate, argument, and protest; all of which is of endless appeal to the Six who has a case to make and is hellbent on winning it.

If he has artistic talent, he may specialize in drawings or paintings awash with self-pity, or having a gallows humour. In one such, done by a Six in prison and entitled *The Lynched Thief's Only Mourner,* a dog raises its head to view the body hanging from the branch of a tree, and howls. In another, an apparition wields a scythe – against whom or what is not shown –, the background of the painting being a blanket of jagged patterning.

One of the cartoons by Charles Bronson, formerly Micky Peterson and dubbed the U.K.'s 'most dangerous inmate', has him manacled in a sealed compartment which a hooded grim reaper with scythe (again!) approaches. Bronson has a Seven subtype; his confined and restrained state denotes loss of liberty.

A Six who felt beyond help made a list of what preoccupied him. He was alone and plagued by voices; having a Five subtype, he may have been a paranoid schizophrenic. Each line but one on the list begins with a sketch of a human face, which alters line by line with the sentiment. On one line he wrote "I am possessed!", and on the head put devil's horns. The last line was "I am not going to make it", and instead of the face he drew the two strokes of a cross.

The mindset of victim, without resentment from being a loser, is one of the desolate Two whose being is dominated by pain and grief. "When you have suffered as much as I have" is the Two speaking, not the Six (nor the Four).

Miscellaneous traits
Of performer e.g. singer, actor: pathos
Contrives situations of danger through uncertainty; tests the
    limits of his fear

Paranoia, as a generalized sense of threat (6-5). For its other
    manifestation, see chapter seven
Satanism (6-5; extends to 5-6)

Misconceptions as to type

It is the Six, and not the Eight, for whom the expression of
anger against himself by someone else can be psychologically
welcome, since on that basis the other person's intentions are
out in the open and removed from the realm of suspicion. He
can use his own anger to antidote his fear.

Passive resistance is a stand of the Six or the Nine. In
the Six, the trait could take the form of a go-slow in protest
– that is, resentment – against job overload, impositions by
management, or demands of employees not met; or a testing
of the boundaries of authority ("In withdrawing cooperation,
how long will it be before I am stopped?"), by the person
whose enthusiasm for the undertaking is lukewarm.

Passive resistance by the Nine is the foot-dragging of
someone who has to give token evidence of action, while
out of stubbornness or laziness he is firmly set against
its completion; 9-1 is the most obstinate subtype on the
Enneagram. The motivation of the Six is to evoke a reaction,
so defining or advancing his position; and of the Nine, a
refusal to budge from where he is and what he is comfortable
with.

Footnote

Further to what is stated under 'Victim/loser mindset', the
remaining adverse psychological factors relating to the Six
and weighing on post-1918 Germany are as follows: the
public sense of having been deceived, for it was not realized
on the home front that by 1918 the army was on the verge
of defeat (betrayal); the abdication and flight of the Kaiser
(abandonment); political polarization to the Left and Right
(loss of a sense of identity); and the hyperinflation of 1923,

and from 1929 the Great Depression (loss of faith in, and respect for, established authority).

On the subject of (self-) respect, those who have dealings with recalcitrant Sixes and who wonder how best to proceed could give thought to some lines of a poem by Dorothy Law Holte:

> "If a child lives with encouragement,
> He learns confidence
> If a child lives with approval,
> He learns to like himself"

Chapter 9

TYPE SEVEN: FREEDOM OF MOVEMENT

Orientation: Against
Outsider state: Negated. Excluded from living: missing out
Primary resonance: TYPE TWO
Secondary resonance: TYPE THREE
7-6:   Freedom of movement has for incentive, or is modified by, social awareness and interaction
7-8:   Freedom of movement is independent and controlling

Comment on name of type
The Seven is defined less by what he does than by how he does it, and especially by the enthusiasm and ease that he brings to his activities and the pleasure that he gains from them, which is what makes the healthy Seven so lively and likeable. Indeed, this non-specific aspect is acknowledged in one of its names, the Generalist. However, it has a dry connotation conveying nothing of enthusiasm: life is as a magnet to the Seven, who is stimuli-driven (see tabulation No.2 in appendix No.I).

If by generalist is meant someone having a wide range of abilities, or whose interests and activities become wide-ranging by one extending to another, the name could loosely fit the Seven; but in the dictionary a generalist is defined as 'one who devotes himself to general studies'. Aristotle (a Five with no subtype) has been described as a generalist; and Thomas Jefferson (see appendix No.4: the Five) would surely be another. In education, a generalist course is for the many what a specialist course is for the few.

The Epicure is another name given to the Seven, which has – misleadingly- a variety of meanings. Certainly there are Sevens who surrender themselves to sensual pleasure: an infamous example from history is the Marquis de Sade; but such a life is very limiting, even a form of imprisonment, hence the antithesis of the freedom with which the type is synonymous.

Although the Seven as epicure and partygoer may indulge his appetite for food and drink, it bears mention that to those for whom the stomach is a boiler to be stoked, eating is a distraction from doing, and not an activity to be savoured or delayed over.

Refinement of taste in food and drink relates primarily to the Four and the Five. The Four's tastes can be exotic or obscure i.e. out of the ordinary; the Five may take care over the purity of food, or enjoy it as a pleasure not derived from human contact. The Seven is hardly the connoisseur: to have before one the very best for tasting may entail an adventure in the procuring but also patience, and the ignoring of all else met with; neither is a trait of the Seven.

Epicurean ethics in their origin are far removed from the sensual indulgence of the term in its modern usage, and without question have more of the Five about them than of the Seven. The teachings hold that pleasure is the only good; and that in its highest expression pleasure is the absence of fear, want, and pain, in a peaceful and self-sufficient state of being. The state is to be preferred to the satisfaction of desires in acts that repeat themselves and are pleasures of the moment. Prudence is extolled, and moderation advocated.

For the rest, the Adventurer is a name that identifies the

Seven, it being understood that life itself is the adventure. A capacity for fun and excitement, eagerness for new experiences, and resourcefulness are all traits of the Seven as adventurer.

I have chosen 'Freedom of movement' as the ideal name for the Seven since it is the polar opposite of the One – and of its constraint. My first thought was for 'Freedom of action', but the name would not encompass the talent of the Seven – bodily, vocal, or aural – for seamless flow of performance in sports, acrobatics, singing, and music. Joe DiMaggio is a Seven with no subtype, Olga Korbut (see 'Life-affirming qualities' below) 7-8, and Frank Sinatra 7-6.

Outsider state

Like the Three and the Eight, with which it shares the orientation 'Against', the Seven transcends the state by force; a process which in its inventiveness (not its motivation) can resemble the Three. For the Seven who succeeds without antagonizing – that is, maintaining the integrity of his enabling qualities as below –, force is insistence and not aggression.

Whether for reasons that are innate or based on social comparison, the Seven in this state feels empty of experiences: excluded from life, at a standstill and not alive. By ingenuity and persistence he discovers remedial ways and means, knowing that if one does not work there are others that can be tried. This is why he is the outstanding organizer (see 'Extension and connection' below), the thought through and the improvised going hand in hand.

He is disarming, fresh in presence, and eager with ideas. To be disarming is to be friendly, artless, and undefensive; to be artless is to have an agenda that does not have to be suspected for motive, nor guessed at. To be defensive is to be distrusting or fearful, self-concerned and perceiving (or misperceiving) of threat; an issue-based and position-taking stance that, being outside the ambit of the Seven, is not his to slow or burden him. Whether or not voiced with confidence, self-deprecation is a disarming trait of the Seven.

It should not be overlooked that unmet security needs in a Seven having a medium or heavy Six subtype will modify the foregoing scenario.

Faced with opposition he is persuasive, not as to his merits or those of what else he is selling (the Three), but as to the granting or restoring of his freedom of movement. As for his weaknesses of character, much is forgiven to someone so likeable.

Life-affirming qualities

The quality with which the Seven who is affirming of life is most blessed is joy. This is not a feeling of joy in life as God-given (the Two), but primarily the expression of joy by achievement, in creative performance in music, song, and physical movement (e.g. ballet, gymnastics). The joy of performing with expertise that which has beauty and grace radiates to the spectator, whose impression is one of delight, even enchantment. Grace, in this physical context, might be defined as beauty in movement. The pleasure-loving propensity of the average Seven has become pleasure-giving. In the Three, the self is validated by achievement; in the Seven, it is life which achievement validates.

Olga Korbut, who at the age of seventeen captivated the world with her performance at the 1972 Olympic Games, is 7-8. For her, "The point of gymnastics was to surprise, amaze and delight. I think that is what I did."

Jacqueline du Pre is 7-6. A supremely gifted cellist who entered music school when she was five, friends remember her as radiant and joyous. At times idiosyncratic, she was said to give her audience "the truth of what she felt." This is not an aesthetic reference to beauty (the Four): what is in evidence is naturalness and skill in a social setting, not the intimacies of privation and consolation, which even if externalized can only be witnessed at a remove.

On the level of the everyday, a joyous outlook in the Seven is gratitude for the good fortune that life has bestowed. The gratitude may be mixed with wonderment, analogous to the child who on his birthday feasts his eyes on the packages awaiting him. Looking to the resonance between the Two and the Seven, the gratitude of the former is towards the source of life; that of the latter, towards the sumtotal of its manifestation. It has been communicated to us that the diversity of life on our planet is for man's enjoyment, with which both types would concur.

His curiosity and openness to experience make the Seven trusting. Risks are taken because awareness of them does not govern decisions; they tend to be made light of or not noticed, or variables could be added to the mode of approach so as to minimize risk by adjustment as the undertaking progresses. The attitude is "I can not wait to do it", not "I can safely do it" (the Six), nor "Having assessed the risk, I know what I can do, and how I should do it" (the Five). In any event, the Seven is the type most liable to have his trust abused, but would assert that the prospect of the experience – or rather, of what would otherwise be forgone – outweighs the risk.

In radiating the warmth that enlivens, the Seven is the nearest thing to a solar type. Again this is complementary to the Two, as the type which by love affirms growth.

Other positive qualities

The traits under this heading are again essentially youth related. It may seem strange to single out resilience as deserving of first mention – but less so in the light of the stresses and strains to which disharmony subjects us, and the benefit of not succumbing to its effects.

Resilience is the strength to spring back to the original state after compression, bending, or stretching: a graphic representation of stresses and strains. In passing, a further indicator of the Seven as polar opposite to the One is the buoyancy of the resilient Seven in contrast to the weight on the shoulders of the duty-bound One. I believe that it is the Seven (7-8) who is best placed to rise above the damage of child abuse.

Pierre-Yves Gerbeau was recruited from Disneyland, Paris as Chief Executive of London's Millennium Dome in February 2000, to revive its appeal; he is a Seven with no subtype. The project had been jeopardized from the start by creative inanity, ministerial meddling, and a hostile press. (Had the Dome been overseen by Fives and Sevens, instead of by a cabal of the image-obsessed and the compliant, the result would have done honour to the year and the U.K.). During the ten months that he was at the helm he refused to be downcast, and made the best of a bad job by turning the attraction into a fun day out, despite resistance to his ideas. Attendance figures improved, and in its last three months of operation the Dome broke even. Everyone took to him. His strenuous efforts to keep the Dome open and to negotiate its purchase were rejected by the government, which for the moment is saddled with its shell.

Tricia Jamal is also a Seven with no subtype. In 1970 she became the first woman foreign exchange broker in London; prior to retirement she was a managing director of a subsidiary of a leading U.K. bank. On her first day as a broker she was told on the phone by an important client, who would not deal with a woman, to "f... off." In the trading room many of the men would turn their backs when she walked in, while others would not speak to her; nor would some clients, aside from the one above. When her probation period was over, "I realized I was good at the work and I was hooked on the excitement of it." The hostility towards her for being a woman increased when she married an Asian man: "One of my biggest clients stopped trading with me simply

140

because he wasn't white." Yet having earned professional respect, on having a daughter she was showered with flowers and champagne!

With resilience, disarmingness (see 'Outsider state' above) is the Seven's passport to inclusion, and an outworking of his trust.

Happiness can go hand in hand with resilience. In a survey of twenty two countries carried out in 2000, Denmark (7-6) was ranked first in having this quality; next came Australia (6-7) and U.S.A. (3- 2). I lack the types of three of the top ten countries, in which with this omission there are two Sevens, two Threes, and two Nines. The ranking of Australia would owe itself to the Seven subtype. Although the sample of countries is small, the findings do correlate with Enneagram theory for the three types highlighted. It should be emphasized that what makes a person happy is not the same from type to type. For the Seven, happiness at its peak is a state of joy; for the Nine (with no peak), a contented state. Whilst success and its acknowledgment bring happiness to the Three, there would seem to be no corresponding state, unless it be satisfaction. A 'sadness index' would yield a predominance of Fours and Sixes.

To have a disarming Seven as head of an undertaking, or leader of a country, when tension or dissent is present is very advantageous. His desire is that no party should feel left out or threatened. Personal connections are accessible to him which others by their attitudes and actions have rendered unuseable by themselves. He knows that to align himself with one side is interpreted as being against another, and that to antagonize is to harden, causing a distancing, the veiling of intent, and the adopting of postures, which is why his allegiances are juggled and on occasion seem wrongheaded, as when one person is the friend of another but will not speak out against the friend's enemy when the resolution of what is at issue matters to all three.

Extension and connection

Life to the Seven is a road atlas covering as large an area as possible, on which wherever he is an array of routes branches out, be they long or short, straight or winding, wide or narrow; he can choose accordingly. Movement is inherent in his designs, and one route can not but connect with another. The one travelled by 7-6 is busier; that of 7-8 is longer and straighter.

Contacts are cultivated, searched out, and noted. They smooth or extend the route, or they could at some point be needed ("One never knows").

An ability to organize is not confined to one class of person, so before considering the Seven its motivation elsewhere can be summarized. The One feels himself to be held accountable for good order. For the Three, organization is a necessity to maintain success by result, and to keep abreast of increased demand. The Five is precise and systematic, so that he understands in any given respect what he is doing. The Six is not a born organizer, but may be so in response to commitment, or to security-consciousness e.g. in having to know for sure where he stands, or in his determination not to be shown up to his peers, both of these stemming from the desire to avoid anxiety.

For the Seven, organization is an exercise in discovering ways and means, and in assemblage. He should have a free hand – and may chafe if he does not. His success arises not so much from greater output (the Three) as from diversified enlargement, as if he were the owner of a building who decides to add on an assortment of extensions. He is in his element coordinating and liaising, these having contact for their mainstay.

Stelios Haji-Ioannou is the founder of easyJet, 'the web's favourite airline', which as at Spring 2001 carried 6.2 million passengers annually; he is 7-6. He does not stand on ceremony; at his own wish he is known as Stelios, the English finding his last name hard to articulate. Add-on businesses to date are easyRentacar, easyValue (where online shopping prices may be compared), easyMoney, and easyEverything (an internet cafe chain). Honest and disarming, he admits that all has not always gone to plan – one of the businesses had to be bailed out from his own resources–, and is aware that "self-deprecation is a way of making yourself liked." At work at company headquarters, he sends out the message that he is accessible by seating himself in a central position in the office. His motivation demonstrates the Six subtype: "I had to prove to myself and the world that I wasn't just the son of a rich father." Constantly on the move (the Seven), he takes four flights a week and stays in hotels for 200 nights a year. 'Easy' is a word instantly identified with the Seven: no worries, no struggle, no delays, no hassle. This is ease in active mode, and has its passive counterpart in the stable Nine who remains at ease by not being affected negatively.

The author who writes rapidly and at length – and the one who is commissioned to write three hundred pages which mushroom to six hundred – is usually a Seven, transported by his enthusiasm for the subject and his desire to entertain the reader, unless he is a Five with a wealth of technical knowledge or one whose literary imagination roams free.

By his centrality (cf. 'solar type' above), the Seven as mediator can tone down or burn away the distrust born of divergent attitudes and goals, building a bridge of hope on to which the parties are encouraged to step, and dared to advance. The term 'mediator' having been allocated traditionally to the Nine, its discussion is covered in chapter eleven.

Work approach

For the One, pleasure should be tinged with work; for the Seven, work should be tinged with pleasure. A young relative of mine who is a Seven was seen to do her school homework perched on the edge of an armchair, conversation going on around her, with half an ear on her radio or CD player, or half an eye on the television.

'Free and easy' says it all; the healthy Seven accomplishes with ease, and is tolerant of distractions. If he is creatively inclined, his mind plays with ideas by free association. Conditions of informality suit him, where rules are few, and allowance is made for routine to be lessened by fresh thinking. He is solution-orientated and, if need be, ingeniously so. In his zest for life he can be indistinguishable from the ambitious Three, and may have to guard against his enthusiasms running ahead of him. In the Seven who works with too broad a brush and can not be succinct, excessive diversification – i.e. venturing into a related area of which he has little knowledge, or finding connections where there are none (see 'Extension and connection' above) – substitutes for expertise.

Limitation and latitude

Authority impacts on the One, the Six, and the Seven. To the One, authority should be obeyed because it is right – and righteous – to do so. To the Six, authority should be obeyed because to keep on its right side – which in the parlance of government is what is meant by 'being on-message' – is to feel secure in the views that he expresses and how he acts; or he tests authority to define what the boundaries are, or in a need for reassurance (e.g. the thought of a youngster towards his parents: "How much am I loved? What if I behave badly?"), these again having a security motivation; or authority is provoked so that he can defend his stand or assert his independence. To the Seven, authority that is perceived to be a bar to action is worn away (erosion) or pushed back (concession) by persuasion and persistence, gone behind the back of, or challenged. The Seven with a medium or heavy Six subtype may also test for boundaries or reassurance.

When a Seven wants permission from a parent that he

suspects will be withheld, he tries to neutralize the ranking of authority, treating the parent as if the two of them were mates. The matter is broached nonchalantly and not decisively ("It's no big deal"). Much is made of facts which would tease out consent, or they are exaggerated; ones which would worry the parent are played down or not mentioned. Casual assurances are given by the Seven, since he does not care for being pinned down too tightly in arrangement. In proportion to the ostensible reasonableness of the request, parental defences are not raised.

The unhealthy Seven takes liberties and bends the rules along the lines of whatever can be got away with. He could be a rogue trader who does every job by halves. He has no time for authority, which he evades or fobs off; nor for regulations and red tape. His attitude to possessions is no better: items that he could do with are pilfered from company premises or building sites, which he justifies to himself with "They can afford it" or "No one will miss it."

Not to know when it is time to stop or step down, as an officeholder or entertainer, is an expression of this category.

Lightness of being

Refrains like "Let's face the music and dance" and "Always look on the bright side of life" are ones that the Seven would endorse. Unpleasant or painful experiences must not mar the enjoyment of life. By understatement or humour they are made light of- or evaded and wished away. Their acceptance is an aspect of resilience (see 'Other positive qualities' above).

Matters which ought to be treated as substantial or serious can be less so to the Seven who has a lightness of being. His humour may be zany, comical, quirky, juvenile, or anarchic. It can be in poor taste, but is not hard-hitting (6-7). He may be a practical joker.

A pathological expression of this trait arises when the demarcation between fact and fantasy is blurred in the mind, which should be distinguished from the conscious substitution of fantasy for fact. The spontaneous liar, with his numerous versions of the 'facts' under interrogation, is a Seven.

Lightness of being can promote irresponsible or fraudulent conduct (see 'Limitation and latitude' above).

Anxiety (7-6)

According to Enneagram literature, an excess of activities (see next heading) is the Seven's method of avoiding anxiety. My own research provides no evidence for this theory. It is the case that anxiety over a matter can create the feeling that he has to busy himself in some activity or other, but that is to react by fending off anxiety with a diversion, and is not sustainable.

One cause of anxiety lies in where as a social being he is positioned: on the inside 'where the action is', or on the outside. An example would be a relationship that ends in bitterness, the partners having enjoyed a joint social life to the full, one of them being 7-6. If their friends felt that the Seven was entirely to blame – and perhaps held the other partner in greater affection anyway – the Seven could find that he or she was now largely friendless.

To be excluded from a social group to which he belonged, without knowing why, causes anxiety ("Why don't they like me?" "What's wrong with me?"). It may be that in his desire not to be alone he is too eager or dictating of the agenda, or that in what he says or does he goes too far, and that he is deaf to hints that others give him about his behaviour. A strong resemblance to the Two may be noted in this feature (see 'Miscellaneous traits' in chapter four).

The Seven is anxious in any situation in which he realizes that he is 'in over his head' but from which he can not extricate himself. Either he will have been too trusting, or he will not have grasped what he has let himself in for. Such Sevens are easy prey to a cult leader (see 'Immaturity' below).

146

Evasion and escapism

A Seven can admit to being homosexual if he feels that he will not lose out by the fact being open knowledge; so it may be kept a secret – strangely for a type whose racier contingent is out at the front in the shameless stakes. If he has a heavy Six subtype he may wonder: "What would they think of me if they knew I'm gay?"; or he may side in safety with the majority (the Six) by passing himself off as contentedly married, or project a robustly heterosexual image.

Liberace is 7-6. A variety performer is of the view that he "manufactured his persona in order to put the persona out on the stage, and not have to go out there himself. And so the showman was born purely in order to hide behind. And a key to this is the enormous lengths to which he would go to make you like him." Until his death, his fans were in ignorance of his homosexuality.

Eve Valois a.k.a. Lolo Ferrari, who died in 2000 aged 30, is also 7-6. She featured regularly on the television programme *Eurotrash* on account of the size of her breasts (54G). She continually had them enhanced because, as she said, "I can't stand life." She went far beyond Liberace in persona manufacture, parading as a freak to be joylessly gawped at, her breasts barricading her real self against the world. Her mother had instilled in her the belief that she was worthless (self-respect: the Six).

As a paedophile (see chapter seven) he has no wish to understand his impulses, and evades having to do so by a bogus rationalizing of them, or by drawing attention away from himself. Many paedophiles deemed untreatable would be found to be self-exonerating Sevens. To quote one, "I don't need any therapy. The way I am is natural. God made me like this. Who are you to try and change me?" For another, the media "brutalize and sexualize our kids everyday."

From inside prison, Kenneth Bianchi – one of the 'Hillside Stranglers' – hatched the idea of turning into reality the storyline of a TV scriptwriter whom he met, whereby she would commit a copycat murder which would prove that he had been wrongly convicted. The plan failed.

There are instances of disintegrated Threes who, having been apprehended after committing a crime, have made statements such as: "How could a normal guy do what I did? It was like another guy inside me", or "It was like it wasn't really me. It was like I was standing somewhere else watching." A Seven could in theory escape into an alternative personality as a refuge from abuse.

Retaliation

Revenge and retaliation being words that are somewhat interchangeable, 'Reactions to being humiliated or denied' in chapter five should be consulted in conjunction with this heading. The trait is not the instinctive and typeless one of tit-for-tat with which anyone might react.

The Seven retaliates by 'returning to the sender' that which is unwelcome. Interestingly, a theme behind what the humiliated Three does is his having been rejected; the Seven, in retaliating, is himself rejecting.

Examples are a Seven who threatened to sue the author of a biography of himself on the grounds that, to judge by the author's literary antecedents, his name would be dragged through the mud (which it was; the threat to sue was not prosecuted); and another who, unsettled by being trailed as a murder suspect, filed a charge alleging harassment and, when someone had a warrant issued for his arrest, a counter-charge alleging an offence against himself (he was in the end charged and found guilty).

Boredom

To be bored, in having nothing to do, is mostly a trait of the Two or the Seven. For the Two the remedy is social involvement, which may be of an annoying kind that taxes the patience. The Seven goes for easy amusements, the mildest of which are escape into, and the excitement of, fantasy; and pranks which annoy and inconvenience, e.g. ringing a door bell then vanishing, or a nuisance telephone call informing an official body of an imaginary incident. What he has done is preparatory to the real fun – a lighting of the fuse, as it were –, and should be complemented by observing the reaction without being seen or apprehended. Over three years a Seven vandalized dozens of library books by humorously doctoring them, put them back in a prominent spot, and watched for the horrified reaction when they were picked up.

If pranks are not fun enough for him, the Seven who is at a loose end torments or tortures animals, or those weaker than himself. The attitude: "Let's see what happens if I/we" in the desire for sadistic excitement, and improvised to lead who knows where, is lethal. As an escape from boredom and not a response to stimuli, this is an incipient expression of a depravity that, if it should prove to be stimuli-generative, could become habitual (see 'Miscellaneous traits' below). The Seven who torments for pleasure should be distinguished from the Three who is a bully, and the Six who does so as a provocation.

Immaturity

In the best of worlds a child is free of cares. The child who can not cope with the thought of outgrowing this world – of having it taken away from him – recoils from the transition to adult, when bodily changes disconcert, the carefree has to be swapped for the responsible, and security is felt to be precarious.

Renowned as a child star to television audiences in the U.K. for her vigorous singing style from the age of nine, Lena Zavaroni is 7-6. She died in 1999, aged 34. Her backstage attendants would unwisely comment on her weight which, consciously or not, she perceived as a prerequisite contingent on which her stay in childhood could be made to last beyond its time. A barrier to integration as an adult was thus raised, and was self-consuming in its effects: an anorexic, her weight sank to four stone. Interviewed in her last years, she was indeed aware of a veil or barrier behind which she subsisted, and which she could not dissolve.

Megalomania

Jean-Bedel Bokassa was self-proclaimed Emperor of the Central African Republic until he was ousted in 1979; he is 7-8. He was infamous for his grotesque excesses, cruelty, and capriciousness. He spent the equivalent of his country's annual gross domestic product on his coronation, fathered 62 children, and by the 1990s was declaring himself to be the 13th Apostle of Christ. He died in 1996. As a point of technical interest, psychic diagnosis reveals that the Eight subtype was not operative. Another example of the disorder is the Roman Emperor Caligula, who is a Seven with no subtype.

Miscellaneous traits

In art: surrealism. Examples are Salvador Dali (Seven with
    no subtype) and Pablo Picasso (7-8)
Bipolar disorder
Depravity that has an adolescent character (excess of
    stimulation, fascination, curiosity), when no one in
    authority is close enough to curb him (7-8 or no subtype)

Misconceptions as to type

7-8 is, in the main, not more but less aggressive than 7-6, because less jostled by interaction. On the other hand, 7-8 is not energized by stimuli competed over.

It should not be taken for granted that the scientist is a Five; he can be a Seven, whose motivation is not the acquisition of knowledge, but the excitement and diversity of the journey of discovery. An example is Galileo, who is 7-6.

Chapter 10

TYPE EIGHT: POWER/ STRENGTH

Orientation: Against
Outsider state: Denied. Without means; held back
Primary resonance: TYPE THREE
Secondary resonance: TYPE TWO
8-7: Energies are released and directed. Outreach of power. Extensive in impact (negatively: rampant)
8-9: Identity and direction are strengthened by consolidation. Concentration of power. Cohesive in impact (negatively: repressive)

Comment on name of type
All three of the names by which the Eight is known – the Leader, the Boss, and the Asserter – have something to commend them, taking into account as they do its dominance.

To assume a position of leadership by force of will does indeed correspond to the Eight. However, this may be arrived at as much by imposition as by consent. By and large, a leader – of a group, organization, or nation – who institutes radical change is not wished for, unless such change is demanded in reaction to stagnation or incompetence, in which case the Eight could find himself accepted unresistingly. It is axiomatic that impact creates disturbance, whereas the preference is to opt for the status quo with improvements.

The forcefulness of the Eight would have to have an outlet if he were chief executive of a company that is trading modestly, homely and staid, and content to remain so. If the company were to appoint him, management and employees would soon live to regret it since many would be out of a job, unwanted in the ethos of dynamism which would mark his tenure.

A successful Eight typically starts out either by building up his own business, or by positioning himself strategically – and, to his employer, indispensably, for his hard work and reliability–, so that in time a controlling role will be within his reach.

In general there are as many leaders who are Threes, Sixes, Sevens, and Nines. Qualities of merit in the Three are self-confidence, enthusiasm, and the projection of an image of success by results; in the Six, soundness of commitment, and a willingness to make a stand for the collective good; in the Seven, enthusiasm (shared with the Three), informality, and the resilience not to bend under adversity; and in the Nine, stability.

As activist, the leader – or ringleader – would mostly be a Six or a Seven; with a sense of idealism, 5-4; or imbued with the epic nature of the struggle, 3-4.

A technical factor which goes against the Boss as a name is that it has no connotation of movement or direction – only one of being in charge.

The Asserter could be the Eight, though the name would equally suit the go-ahead Three or the disputatious Six.

Outsider state

To be denied is the Eight's outsider state, and is countered by the will to rise above and to prevail over. In the Three, the Eight's point of primary resonance, the state has a social dimension and is for want of acceptability of worth; in the Eight, it has a survivalistic dimension and is for want of

152

strength. Because survivalism is the primal mode of existence, the hazards of life and physical infirmity are experienced and endured without much being made of them.

To be without means is to be powerless. The way forward is in self-reliance, tenacity of belief in self-empowerment, working indefatigably, the accumulation of resources, and alertness to circumstance.

To be held back is a state of restraint and of energies in latency, like an arrow that is pulled back in the bow before being let go. Release is a breaking free and bursting forth, with a momentum to travel great distance over a destined path.

Having begun drafting this chapter, the name of a person whose fame lay in sensational demonstrations of the symbolism of the outsider state came to my mind: the legendary Houdini, who is 8-7. In one feat, he was shackled with chains and placed in a locked and roped packing case which was lowered into a river. In another, he was suspended upside down in a straitjacket 75 feet above ground.

Modalities of strength

Energy, breadth of coverage, and diversification are to 8-7 what mass, centralization, and standardization are to 8-9.

As the modernizer, 8-7 responds to that which is in need of impetus, by reformulating and reinvigorating; 8-9, to that which is in need of unifying and planning, being disparate and without defined identity.

Specific strengths are the taking charge of personal destiny, in an act of karmic reparation; and to overcome against what would be thought to be insurmountable odds.

Aspects of the absolutist are the quest in 8-7 for perfection or totality of representation, as coach, film director, or writer; and in 8- 9 the cornering of a market sector, or Mafia tactics. The film director Stanley Kubrick is 8-7, in which respect it should be noted that the social control exerted by such an

Eight is never an end in itself – a contrast with the Three – but is incidental to the perfection of the finished product, which fails if its assemblage is loose. The director of *The Exorcist*, William Friedkin, is an 8-7 who on set was not only exacting but ruthless in what he subjected the actors to. "Of course I was mortified when theatre owners had to call ambulances or swab the aisles", he has said, "but I was delighted too. It showed that we'd gotten through. The film's an assault."

Strength of character should not be confused with a show of strength and its accoutrements. John Wayne is widely taken to be an Eight, but is in fact 6-7. His movie persona talks and acts tough, laying down the law as dictated by his rugged outlook; but what would he be without a gun? His manner would be blustering but not intimidating.

The psychology of power is a weapon of the Six (but see 'Control' below). The Eight relies on the means he has at his disposal, not on incapacitating his opponent with an attitude based on figuring out what is in his mind in order to disconcert him.

Specific strengths

Elaborating on the two expressions of strength introduced under the previous heading, Madame H.P. Blavatsky, a co-founder of the Theosophical Society, is an Eight with no subtype but with an admixture of the Five, and an example of taking charge of personal destiny. She was the agency through whom the preparatory instalment of three interpretations of the Ageless Wisdom was given out to the world between 1875 and 1890. The second or intermediate in the series was transcribed by Alice A. Bailey between 1919 and 1949, whilst the third or revelatory one is expected ere long in this century. Alice Bailey dedicates *A Treatise on Cosmic Fire* to Mme. Blavatsky, "that great disciple who lighted her torch in the East and brought the light to Europe and America in 1875." In her *Discipleship in the New Age* Val. II, the statement is made that "the harm done to the Ashram of the Master Morya by H.P.B. in his earlier incarnation as Cagliostro, is only now fading out, and its repercussions affected the whole Hierarchy" (pp.331-2). Cagliostro died in 1795; Mme. Blavatsky was born in 1831. Cagliostro is 3-4, the subtype most connected with black magic.

Mother Teresa, founder of the Missionaries of Charity, appears to be another such example; she is 8-9. The word 'charity' suggests the Two (2-1 or 1-2); yet charity does not market itself in the style of an American business (the Three), still less by lobbying the leaders of nations. A home for the dying is of the nature of the Five. In short, these indications have no consistency.

Her faith in providence and her asceticism point to the One or the Five, but her uncomplaining assent to the role of decorated and saintly celebrity does not; nor does the odd blend of love and autocracy, or the outspoken naivety of her social ideas set against the Order's secretiveness. She affected a lack of knowledge of the vileness of certain regimes, as if that were an area of life outside her cognizance, which is explainable by the Nine subtype in its 'ostrich' tendency of not seeing what it does not want to. No conclusion can be drawn from the level of patient care; some volunteers come away impressed and changed for life by the gentleness of spiritual solace administered, yet others report a depersonalized, even production line attitude.

She is a rare example of someone who can not be assessed on the facts alone.

The following two quotations might be said to have a flavour of the One and the Two but are misleading, since the speaker is not the sufferer. To a patient with terminal cancer, "You are suffering like Christ on the Cross. So Jesus must be kissing you." "It is very beautiful for the poor to accept their lot, to share it with the passion of Christ." Her view on abortion is cranky and undiscriminating, confirming the influence of the Nine; in her speech on being awarded the Nobel Prize in 1979 she said, "I feel that the greatest destroyer of peace today is abortion. Because it is a direct war, a direct killing – direct murder by the mother herself   If a mother can kill her own child – what is left but for me to kill you and you to kill me? – there is nothing in between." On a visit to London she remarked, "I say to the women of Calcutta: 'Have as many children as you want!'"

Her vocation was shaped by faith; a goal-driven and unshakeable conviction of destiny (the Eight); and self-surrender, classed as a virtue in Eastern thought, and in its absolutism in keeping with the Eight. Self-surrender may be the quality which, in conjunction with her status, made her paradoxically both so humble and so powerful. The opening of homes in many countries argues for a Seven subtype, until it is remembered that judged alongside modern drugs and medical technology, the Order's facilities are basic.

Jonathan Nobles was executed by lethal injection in Texas in 1998. In the 1980s, having taken drugs and alcohol, he had stabbed to death two women. As a child, he was sexually abused by both his parents, savagely beaten, and from the age of five repeatedly attempted suicide. He is 5-6, and during his years on death row integrated to the Eight. For eight years he and a woman living in England, Pam Thomas, were in correspondence, in increasing trust and understanding of each other. In due course his violence and bravado abated. He would perform acts of kindness for newer inmates, and wrote of his horror at not being able to atone for his crimes.

He asked if Mrs. Thomas could be with him at his execution; shocked and frightened, she replied that she would. Two weeks before the date, with a mediator he and the mother of one of his victims had a lengthy meeting in the prison, at which he apologized and took responsibility for what he had done, and was forgiven by the mother, at which he was quite overwhelmed. Prior to the session he had written to Mrs. Thomas, "It would be a very beautiful thing if all the hate, anger and misery which I have brought into this world in the past 36 years could be tossed upon that gurney and die with me. Beautiful, because then there would be more room in this world for love, joy and peace." When the hour of his execution arrived, from behind the glass partition he greeted the victims' families in turn, apologizing from the bottom of his heart and saying he hoped that they could find peace. He recited the 13th chapter of the First Epistle of Paul to the Corinthians, then greeted his few intimates, Mrs. Thomas among them, and began to sing *Silent Night* as unconsciousness and death bore him away.

An example of national reparation is the Truth and Reconciliation Commission, set up in South Africa (8-9) in 1996 to draw a definitive line under the dark years of repression and reprisal, not by the administration of justice and sentence carried out (the One), but by the personal confronting of the facts, in what would be "a much more detailed and credible picture of torturers, murderers and victims than any previous investigations anywhere in the world", to quote Nelson Mandela's biographer, Anthony Sampson. In the context of totality of representation (see 'Modalities of strength' above), truth is one of the faces of reality, and its uncushioned admission an act of self-liberation.

Germany and Switzerland (see appendix No.5) do not fall in this category in respect of reparation for Nazi persecution, procedures having been drawn out over decades, inevitably with much legal and bureaucratic intervention along the way.

Catherine Cookson is 8-7 and someone who overcame against all the odds. She died in 1998, having sold by then some 100 million copies of her 80 novels. A third of the top 100 titles borrowed from libraries throughout the 1990s were hers. She had to break through a succession of barriers of disadvantage. Her mother was an alcoholic. As a youngster she felt stifled by the squalor of a community where horizons

157

were stunted by the daily grind. The stigma of her illegitimacy, which was known to her schoolmates, shamed and haunted her. She had an inherited blood disease which caused continual haemorrhaging and anaemia, and a mental breakdown lasting for years after four miscarriages. In the foreword to *Our Kate* she exorcized her stigma, exposing it to the gaze of her readership with a self-defying courage, in writing that "my cure would never be complete unless I could openly associate myself with two words, two words that had been my secret shame for so long, namely, 'illegitimate' and 'bastard'". Her locality was the inspiration for her raw material, and she did not recoil from transporting her reader to scenes of the grimmest reality.

I find Henry Kissinger to be an Eight with no subtype but with admixtures of the Five and Six. Lauded on his death by Western leaders, he had however an infinitely darker side.

During the Vietnam War, he and then-President Nixon ordered clandestine bombing raids on neutral Cambodia, in an effort to flush out Viet Cong forces in the east of the country.

For context, the U.S. dropped more than two million tons of bombs on Cambodia from 1965 to 1973 – marginally less than the tonnage dropped in the whole of the Second World War – including Hiroshima and Nagasaki.

Cambodia was left destabilized, and into the power vacuum would come Pol Pot and the Khmer Rouge.

Control

We have heard much of control freakery by the 'New' Labour government. This has nothing to do with the Eight, but is the control by undue influence of the Three: micro-management (see 'Orientation by result' in chapter five), the stifling of debate and dissent, and the misrepresentation of results that amount to less than what was promised, or their suppression, in order to maintain an impression of unspoiled success.

Control by the Eight may be illustrated by the mode of operation in business. Aside from matters of routine, what is not done by him is entrusted to those whose loyalty he believes by experience or recommendation to be solid, and who respect (? fear) him; they are extentions of his will. Such loyalty is a necessity, since the strength of the business could be put at risk if a valued employee had a loose tongue or defected to a competitor. He insists on an optimal performance from his employees; they are a workforce single-mindedly focused on the goal. Intimidation is used if disloyalty looms. The ideal employee for such an Eight would be a loyal Six.

Power may be wielded economically, by the acquisition of means (e.g. executive post, wealth, market share); or psychologically, by taking possession of others' space, rendering them subservient. The business magnate as an Eight belongs in the former class, the dictator in either, and the racketeer in both.

Not to be confused with this form of power is the authority that stems from force of personality, which is less an attribute of the Eight than of the first ray (see the teachings of Alice Bailey on the Seven Rays). That said, the powerful Eight often has a first ray component in the mentality or personality. In case of doubt, what is under consideration is: does his commanding or intimidating presence owe itself more to his manner (first ray) or to what he has at his disposal?

Power of means, released as an excess of force, is the equivalent in the Three, and carries a subtext of the desire to impress.

The psychological wearing down of a victim is accomplished by manufacturing a climate of threat. The strategy should be distinguished from that of the Six. An Eight can not always carry out what he threatens either.

With disintegration to the Five, the climate of threat

159

becomes one of terror. No one is above suspicion; traitors and saboteurs are felt to be everywhere, in a state calling to mind the paranoid 6-5. A false sense of security may be induced by heightening tension only to lower it temporarily, or the person may be kept in suspense.

Control may also be a self-aggrandizing indulgence. A guest of James Goldsmith, an 8-9, who spent a weekend with him at his Mexican palace, reported that her "sense of being surrounded was very strong; the sense of discreet, total control at Quixmala was almost surreal. Anywhere I sat, my half-empty glass would be full next time I looked, and much later, when I returned to my perfectly appointed villa, I was startled to see my hairbrush had been meticulously cleaned, my make-up bag zipped closed, my clothes hung up, and the fruit basket, from which I'd taken a few grapes before leaving, entirely replenished."

Social manner

Life, to the Eight, is not for negotiating one's way through, but for forcing one's way through. He does not overcome opposition by weight of argument or charm, but by strength of will and means.

The manner is direct and uncompromising. Some Eights are soft-spoken (usually 8-9); others are forceful even when sensitivity would be indicated, which should not be construed as being talked down to or lectured.

Pride

For the Eight, pride is an interior sentiment of worth, not a social badge, and rests on self-reliance, the strength of character to overcome and not to yield or be sidetracked, and achievement of the goal. In its classical expression, the trait belongs to the fearless warrior and conqueror who would be held in awe for the mightiness of his deeds.

Although it is the proud Eight who may not forgive the

breaking of a code of honour, the person for whom conduct judged to have brought shame on the social unit should be avenged is a Six, his concern being that its ties and traditions must be upheld. To the Eight, the offence is one of weakness; to the Six, one of disrespect and noncompliance.

Unforgivingness

It is prudent not to have an Eight for an enemy. Insults to the person or the family name, underhand behaviour, or disloyalty can be very badly received. Underhand behaviour especially wounds the pride and rouses to anger, since it preempts open combat. Tiny Rowland, who created the £2 billion Lonrho conglomerate, is 8-9. He never forgave Mohamed al-Fayed (3-4) for acquiring Harrods, less perhaps because it was the prize which he most coveted, than for al-Fayed having outsmarted him in his provision of funding for the purchase. In like fashion, Catherine Cookson erased from her autobiography all mention of a childhood friend and her family, the friend having gossiped against her. To sever contact by disinheriting is another expression of the trait.

Lust for power

To possess is the ultimate form of control, which to the Eight means conquest and subjugation.

Abduction may have a financial motive, or a psychological one, in the satisfaction of having the power of life and death over the victim, in a master:slave relationship.

The fearsome extreme throughout history of the lust for power is those individuals in positions of command who would rampage over a territory with their troops. One such is Ezzelino da Romano. In 1227 he besieged and entered Padua; it is estimated that over the next twenty years a quarter of the city's inhabitants were executed on his orders. Not content simply to murder his victims, many were tortured and mutilated, in Padua and elsewhere, for which he was excommunicated by the Pope in 1248.

Stalin, an adept in the promulgation of fear and 8-9, is an exponent in the modern-day and ideological setting. It may be wondered whether, as the architect of the industrialized Soviet state, he was motivated firstly to this end, or by the lust for power.

Misconceptions as to type

There is a widespread notion that the Eight is the defender of the weak. My findings provide no evidence of the trait. Why would someone for whom conscience is not a prime quality, and who personifies strength and self-reliance, have sympathy for the weak? To move forward is the natural mode of the Eight, whereas defence is a mode that is stationary – or, if failing, retrograde – and security motivated (the Six). Moreover, to fight others' battles for them is to submit to an external agenda: something that no Eight would ever do. The lad at school who defends smaller children against the bully is typically 6-7; he thereby proves himself and is psychologically secure, rights an injustice, is regarded as a responsible member of the school, and earns respect – that most coveted of qualities for the Six –, even admiration.

On the questionable basis that the Eight is high-minded, some authorities ascribe justice and magnanimity to it. As a universal value whose lack is an unconscionable defect, justice relates to the One; as an ideal or as harmony, to the Five (with a Four subtype or none); and as a minority issue, to the Five (5-6), the Six, or the Seven (7-6).

Magnanimity is the spirit of forgiveness that by goodwill lessens or annuls an antagonism. Being disarming, the trait is mainly one of the Seven. Allied to a need for moderation amidst the problematical, magnanimity can be a gesture of the pragmatic Five.

Strength and weakness as a pairing, and the mind games

that decide who has which, are a preoccupation of the Six. The Eight could not care less about hierarchy within the peer group, angling for attention as the leader, insisting that he be stood up to, and so on.

If he has to submit to the course of his life being decided for him against his wishes, the correlation is with the Eight, the state being one of absolute denial. On an evening in June 2001 Crown Prince Dipendra of Nepal, who is 8-7, shot fourteen members of his family; the King and Queen, with ten others, died. In 1989 he had visited the U.K., where he was introduced to Devyani Rana, of whom he would remark to a relative, "She's the only woman I'm going to marry." For her part his mother compiled her own shortlist, regarding the choice as hers to make, and advised her husband that there were only two women in the Kingdom suitable to becoming Crown Princess; Devyani was not one of them. Being headstrong and accustomed to being deferred to, Dipendra had "always got what he wanted", as Devyani's brother Gorakh put it. In the view of a newspaper editor, however, his mother "was not above using pressures of opposition to try and get family members to do things the way she wanted them." It was felt by many that she feared being pushed aside. A year before the massacre, Dipendra had announced to the astonished family that he would marry Devyani, and if prevented they would bear the consequences.

Footnote

The attributes of the outsider state – i.e. to be without means or held back- should be understood in absolute and not relative terms, otherwise the correlation will not be with the Eight. Thus the person who is determined to leave behind disadvantaged circumstances, and the impaired self-worth of feeling that he is not the equal of others, by proving himself in the wider world – which could be competitively, or with an element of "I'll show them!" – is a Seven (7-6). His incentive is the realization of what he is missing out on and excluded from (the Seven), in a world hitherto inaccessible to him but to which he is now resolved to belong (the Six).

Chapter 11

TYPE NINE:
THE FUNDAMENTAL
AND UNCHANGING

Orientation: Away from
Outsider state: Estranged. Need for something to identify with
Primary resonance: TYPE FOUR
Secondary resonance: TYPE ONE
9-8:   The strength of the unchanging. Deep-rootedness of attitude and habit
9-1:   The unchanging imbued with legitimacy. "It has always been so, therefore it is right"

Comment on name of type

The names given to the Nine, the Peacemaker and the Mediator, are misnomers resulting from the unthinking use of the word 'peace', and should be abandoned. The Nine is indeed peaceable: his concern is with a peaceful environment in which to live; he has none with reconstructing a peace which has been broken by others, whether or not it was his too.

Peacemaking is a complex and unpredictable process – traits that are foreign to the Nine –, varied in momentum and direction by the twists and turns of what is insisted on, proposed, bargained over, or ruled out. The good nature of the Nine does not equip him to handle the accusing or the intransigent, the angry or the excitable; nor can he finesse his actions.

A Nine as peacemaker would have patience, and the desire not to make a bad situation worse. He would play down differences, and would not wish to disagree with anyone. Issues would not be tackled thoroughly, since the more they were, the more differences would emerge. A vague consensus would be cobbled together and before long probably come apart, or resolution would be deferred.

One reason for the Nine's approach may be seen in its orientation 'Away from', shared with the Four and the Five. In the Five, the orientation operates from a position of detachment and distance, and is specific. In the Nine, the position is reversed, being one of non-specific association and proximity, with a perspective that is subject to being influenced more than it brings influence to bear.

The peacemaker is likely to be a Five who is disinterested, accustomed to figuring out move and countermove, and can restore reason by his calm and measured language; or a Seven who by his ease of manner has the antagonists lowering their defences and connecting with each other out of mutual need.

Outsider state

In being estranged, the Nine has a vegetative existence in an abstract world within himself, because he does not identify with anything. Identity is based on sameness, not as conformity (the Six), but as an affinity with, or sense of oneness with, by virtue of environmental or circumstantial association with whatever or whoever most impresses itself upon him.

If his identity is rooted in a belief, there is no for-or-against polarity or tension (the Six); rather it is as if he is contentedly domiciled in, and lives through, the belief. The theme of domicile is a psychological key to the Nine and, as will be seen, manifests itself in various forms.

Fundamental qualities

Of the positive qualities of the Nine stability is the one comprising, as it were, the soil wherein all others flourish. The United Kingdom is 9-1, and will be returned to more than once in this chapter. Commenting on the menace that he felt Diana, Princess of Wales, posed to the monarchy, a reader wrote to a newspaper that "Monarchs deal in eternal values, continuity and tradition. They are like ballast in a ship. They keep the ship of state upright and stable"; and that "Although they should reflect current moods, their role is essentially conservative." The word 'ballast' may be paused at; it is a reminder that stability has the attribute of weightedness, which holds firm against being imperilled – or prevents itself from adaptation.

The social strengths of stability are exemplified in a British television character of decades ago: the village policeman, Dixon of Dock Green. He was 'part of the scenery'; his presence was familiar, amiable, dependable, and trusted – old-fashioned qualities conveying comfort and reassurance: the notion that things are as they should be, and will continue to be so.

Homeliness has, for the Nine, a subtext of safety, in the shunning of that which would diminish the values of decency and probity; or, in a word, that which is unwholesome. In the Six – the security point on the Enneagram – danger is foreseen and confronted; in the Nine, impropriety and nastiness are stayed away from and shielded against. Gene Autry, 'the singing cowboy', is a Nine who integrated to the Three, and someone who projected the homely image at its best. As an obituary stated, "So unviolent and morally spotless were his films that whole families used to go to them; never has a Hollywood cowboy been so popular with very young children and middle-aged women." His 'ten cowboy commandments' advocated fair play, truthfulness, patriotism, respect for women and the elderly, and racial and religious tolerance. He knew his audience not as a Three does in marketing himself, but because his values were theirs; as he said, "I'm just an average guy. That's why I knew what average guys and gals of my generation were like." His business empire embraced five music companies – he made more than 600 recordings and wrote some 200 songs –, a touring rodeo, a television corporation, a baseball team, and huge real estate holdings. Three years before his death in 1998, his fortune was estimated at $320 million.

Autry's fair play is often cited as a British quality, and could be defined as justice tempered by what is fitting and harmonious. The quality has surprising applications in 'doing the decent thing' towards another. The escape across the English countryside of two handsome pigs of a prized breed en route to the abbatoir received nationwide media coverage. Popular sentiment decreed that having made a gallant bid for freedom they should be spared, and they were duly sent to an animal sanctuary.

Another such performer was Perry Como, a Nine (9-1) who also integrated to the Three. As he said, and so typically for the type, "True happiness is found in simplicity and contentment."

And like Autry, the principles of good taste and family values were fundamental to him.

"Perhaps the reason people rarely talk about his formidable attributes as a singer is that he makes so little fuss about them. That celebrated ease of his has been too little understood. Ease in any art is the result of mastery over its craft. You get them together to the point where you can forget how you do things and concentrate on what you are doing. Como is known to be meticulous about rehearsing the material for an album. The hidden work makes him look like Mr. Casual." From an album cover note.

Updating to the present, to quote from a news source in relation to Charles' cancer shock, "the Queen has been a rock for the King during his toughest test".

I find Camilla to be 9-8. In this role, steadfast and unwavering are two words which come to mind.

Two of her personal interests are said to be horticulture and gardening – both can be pursuits of the Nine, being of the countryside.

Contentment and simplicity are two traits which may be examined as one. As with so much else that is creditable about the Nine, they tend to be underrated. It was pointed out in chapter three that for at least one school of thought these qualities rank as virtues.

In its purest expression, contentment is a lasting and even state of mind whose only demand is for the meeting of basic wants and freedom from disharmony, and which is otherwise cheerily accepting of life as it is. Being effortless, contentment could arise from putting to use a natural endowment (e.g. as entertainer), but not from striving after a goal or possessively. Unlike happiness, contentment is contained, not giving notice of itself or overflowing.

What links simplicity to contentment is that both 'make do' with what is foremost to hand, in idea as in action ("Let's keep it simple"). The cause of complexity in human affairs is the individualism of thought; Wittgenstein refers to 'the knots in our thinking' which the philosopher attempts to unravel. Individualism spells separation from, not association with – the complex, in thought or execution, has few adherents –, and as such means nothing to the Nine.

Surveys indicate that the level of contentment in the U.K. is not what it once was, despite an unprecedented prosperity. The reasons lie in the radical changes which, since the late 1900s, have been undergone: fragmentation of the social fabric (dissociation); the erosion of staple industries (loss of continuity); modernization of working practices (disorientation); job insecurity (loss of contentment); and a steep decline in respect for the authority of our institutions (dissociation). Also at issue is the effect of a culture of consumerism on the values of contentment and simplicity!

Independence and the exercising of choice and 'rights' are now the norm, which does not remotely sit well with the other-directedness of the Nine. Most affected is the family, in ties weakened or broken (dissociation). Relationships which in times past were deemed to carry social and moral obligations are discarded if ungratifying, or are casually entered into – the U.K. is reported to have one of the highest divorce rates in Europe; and almost a third of absent fathers pay no child support.

When the U.K. was a class society (see 'Class and caste' below), a person's standing and employment were decided for him in terms of the social stratum in which he was brought up. Phrases like the prospective "Your place is in/with"; the imperious "Keep him in his place"; the indignant "I know my place"; and the deferential "It's not my place to tell you this, but" are a relic of those days.

Time constraints do not figure in the life-pattern of the Nine, which is why another positive quality is patience. A Nine could excel in teaching on an elementary level what needs much repetition to be assimilated, or in experimenting at a trade or craft until the right way of proceeding is discovered. The trait is painstaking but not complex (the Five).

Sense of identity

Identity gained by association with those around him is the line of least resistance for the Nine. He pervades with his presence as a resource of continuity and dependability. In helping mode he has to be distinguished from the Two (see 'The Nine and the Two' below). On her retirement, a teacher of infants who is single and a Nine made a new life for herself as carer to her elderly and frail parents, with whom she lived, and as a general helper to their large number of relations, in each of whom she took a kindly and generous interest. This extended family was practically the sumtotal of her world. A letter that she wrote to a friend covered ten or twelve pages, in a nonstop narrative detailing the day-by-day news of the family and her part in it, her style a throwback to the cinema newsreels of long ago in which the commentator would flit breezily from one item to the next.

The position of the above ex-teacher is satisfactory, since her world will always exist. Less so was that of a Nine who for 51 years lived for and through her husband – until his death. Thereupon her world collapsed and she vegetated aimlessly, her habit of participating in everything with him having no outlet. She had had pursuits of her own, which very unwisely she let fall away as her life meshed increasingly with his.

Other unchanging areas of life which can be associated with in identity are the natural world and religion. A Nine who is a botany and zoology graduate asked me, "Do you know why I like trees?" The answer could be guessed: "Because they are always there." The type might delve into the past, in tracing the history of something with which he has grown to have close contact.

A country's sense of identity may be in its heritage of preserved customs and structures, if in value they have not been overtaken by modernity. Of this, India is an example.

For the moment, the U.K. is at a crossroads in identity. To some, the country is stuck in a 'We won the war' time-warp; to others, we are dithering with our half-in, half-out policy towards Europe. Our apprehensions over monetary union stem from the event being of necessity a radical change overnight. By nature the Nine responds to major change by acclimatizing slowly or in stages. The governing factor is the attribute of weightedness alluded to earlier: the more satisfactory his existing state is to the Nine, and the more he is habituated to it, the less reason he has to change. At present, the U.K. economy is flourishing.

Clubs, as associations of the like-minded for the enjoyment of their pursuits, are a favoured social inclination of the Nine. They should be friendly, leisurely, non-political, and if competitive unaggressively so.

One of the causes of nostalgia is the fear of change. In the U.K. there is a sentimentalized nostalgia for the 'good old days' of communities where everybody knew everyone else, the front door was not locked, the side street was a playground, and a neighbour would pop round to borrow some bread or sugar and be told the latest gossip. This is a conception of the community as its sumtotal of homes, safe and cosy, and shielded from the world outside (see 'Fundamental qualities' above).

Occupations

If changes of trend and fashion, peer group awareness, and personal ambition are removed from everyday living, what remains is the domain of the Nine: the fundamentals which can not be done without. This means basic foodstuffs and household items, and essential services (e.g. general store, newsagent, grocery, utility industries, transport, health, sundry office tasks). Computerization has its uses for the Nine as part of an automated process.

Many Nines live and work in the countryside or are craftsmen. The countryside provides for unchanging needs, not the ever-changing wants of manufactured consumer demand and of a technology constantly updating and complexifying itself amidst a limitless information flow (the Five and the Seven) – all to the supposed ends of making life simpler by easing the workload and speeding up the throughput. At this point the qualities of contentment and simplicity might be reviewed (see 'Fundamental qualities' above).

Crafts are to the Nine what art is to the Four (see tabulation No.7 in appendix No.I). The craft of the Nine is governed by

172

practical usage and tradition. Its skill is developed through familiarity with the material, by repetition and patience. (The Arts and Crafts Movement would seem to be a decorative bridge between the Four and the Nine, and to relate to the Five).

His expertise is not confined to crafts. He could be a repair man, conversant with every possible malfunction in a given appliance, as well as with the workings of older or obsolete models, and have handy hints as to maintenance; or the person who, with simple equipment, unblocks drains or sweeps chimneys. He could have an unsurpassed knowledge of local history or features.

Class and caste

We are assured that the U.K. of today is a classless society, despite the currency of the term 'middle-class'. What is certain is that the determination of our society by class has vanished, swept away by universal access to education and raised aspirations. However, a rump of the class system persists wherever advancement is secured by privilege, and via the 'old boys' network' of social connection and recommendation.

The British class system fostered identity with a given social stratum, and sameness of socio-economic outlook. An expectation was placed by society on the citizen as to his field of employment or service (the One; the other possible correlation would be with the Six), whether professional, labouring, or menial.

This heading does not have reference to feudalism, nor to the days when England was a Three (see appendix No.5).

Two types of countries which may be contrasted with 9-1 in its social hierarchy are the Five and the Seven. Social standing is not a factor for the Five, who is the egalitarian and whose social awareness may not extend much beyond himself. The Seven treats authority and rank lightly or, if he is the one to have them, wears them lightly. Women have the greatest equality in countries which are Sevens.

India is also 9-1. Its caste system, laid down in ancient Vedic teachings and, for many, unchanging (the Nine), regulates Hindu society and is, to quote an Indian human rights organization, "India's social reality." In the view of a spokesman for the World Hindu Council, "Caste, the feeling that each one performs his duty, has kept the country and society together." Each layer of society is preserved, which includes the avoidance of 'contamination' from lower castes (not the Five but the One, this form of contamination being deemed to be ethically wrong, not invasive of a person's space). The justice (the One) of the system, which condemns a fifth of India's population to lives of poverty and degradation, has a philosophical logic; namely, that it must be karmically right for someone to be born into the caste to which he belongs, and that obedience (the One or the Six) to its customs will lead to rebirth into a higher caste (the self-improvement ethos of the One). The anthropological rationale of the caste system is the imposition of stability and order on cultural diversity within a single society.

Half measures

Being by nature peaceable and well disposed towards everyone, the Nine tends to avoid disagreement or making decisions that others might not go along with. For the Nine who is in a position of authority, to allow a half measure is to substitute tacit agreement for a decision. Underlying issues are present which, if brought to the surface, would cause division or even an impasse, putting a stop to the smooth continuity that he would wish to preserve. In an 'ostrich' posture he does not raise them, having no idea of how they should be dealt with, and hopes that a consensus will eventually emerge. Expressions like 'to look the other way' and 'not to rock the boat' come to mind; the latter could also

174

refer to the Six (see 'Assessment of type' in chapter one, in relation to procrastination).

The half measure should not be confused with the token measure (see 'The comfort of continuity' below).

Lack of assertion

The unassertive Nine will have been undemanding as a youngster, doing what was suggested for him, tagging along with friends, or wandering off in the neighbourhood. He may have been pushed into the background by those with a stronger presence, and will not have objected. His pastimes were uncomplicated and involved no call upon his parents; they are exemplified by the enjoyment of the sights and sounds of the summer countryside, bathed in the warmth of the sun (the same sensation as lazing in a hot bath), when he would lose both himself and track of time.

As an adult, his sentiments go unexpressed; or else they are not his own, being a mishmash of those that by their force or repetition he has absorbed.

The comfort of continuity

There is an armoury of methods by which the Nine insulates himself against change. The untidy accumulation of anything and everything is effectively a declaration: "Here I am, and here I stay." The weightedness has become a dead weight. A tell-tale sign is piles of old newspapers; any family may have a week or two's worth of them – the Nine may have them feet high. Things are not got rid of; they are gone over in a desultory way and in the process intermixed, or put aside for sorting or resorting. As a Nine said to me, in a quaint under-statement, "I don't mind things higgledy-piggledy." Mail yet to be actioned, opened or not, disappears into sundry heaps, much time being spent in its retrieval.

Continuity is ensured by procrastination, tokenism, obfuscation, and the 'ostrich' posture whereby he tunes out of his awareness what he does not want to know about.

Procrastination takes at least three forms. Deadlines are dealt with by ignoring them until the eleventh hour, then rushing into action to produce an outcome that is third-rate, no time or thought having been devoted to it. Trivial matters are toyed with, whereas ones of pressing importance receive no attention. 'A stitch in time saves nine' is a motto that is not heeded; a matter that is low priority may not be so years later. The 'ostrich' posture is all-purpose and may be resorted to in conjunction with procrastination, or separately from it.

Tokenism is the measure that substitutes for completion from the resistant Nine who has been driven to acknowledge that something has to appear to be being done. By being tinkered with, tasks are always ongoing and never concluded.

An expression of tokenism in the U.K. is the routine holding of a formal enquiry following incidents such as a serious transport accident, or a murder by a paranoid schizophrenic who should by then have been hospitalized or who was released prematurely, the purpose of the enquiry being less to clarify and strengthen procedures than to 'kick the matter into the long grass', with deliberations that are spun out inordinately – even for years –, and subsequent recommendations largely unimplemented.

Obfuscation is obstructive resistance. What started out as a clear cut issue is clouded by the indeterminate or half-unaddressed, or meanders in train of thought or argument into incidentals and the irrelevant. For those implicated, this trait is exasperating and a recipe for tangled lines of communication, delay, and wasted effort. It can be wilful and retaliatory.

Lack of discrimination
Besides being in two structural relationships, the Eight, Nine, and One share a trait, in the unwillingness to deal in shadings of value judgment, so that something is either right or wrong without consideration of broader views. In the Eight, force of

endeavour is rendered all the stronger; in the One, deviation from what is seen as right is averted. In the Nine the trait is passive, and is given rise to when an idea impresses itself upon the mind with a head-on immediacy which blots out shadings. Acceptance of the idea is unquestioning, and its articulation stubbornly simplistic.

A national manifestation of the trait was the reaction in the U.K. to the death of Diana, Princess of Wales, which was also striking for the protractedness of its fervour. She was instantly elevated to the rank of an 'icon' (the word has been contemporarily degraded into denoting a mega-celebrity, but is in origin the representation of a sacred personage), and conversely Prince Charles was demonized; she could do no wrong, and he could do no right. It was as if the torrent of prurient newsprint about her, for years so eagerly devoured by her 'admirers', had never appeared. In a further distortion, sentiments of national shock blurred into ones of resurrected personal grief and victimhood through emotional over-identification (the Nine); thousands who had not set eyes on Diana felt, by association with her pain, that they knew her. In its herd instinct, the phenomenon would have been readily entered into by Nines; and in its dramatic and tragic aspect, by Twos.

Another topical example from the U.K. is the campaign over paedophiles which was activated after the abduction and murder of eight-year-old Sarah Payne in 2000, during which the homes of several people, presumed guilty but in fact innocent, were attacked. In language that is equally suited to the death of Diana, a journalist commented, "We want to be close to tragedy, while remaining far off. We want to experience it as if it is our tragedy too; our loss, when, of course, it isn't." This is because for some Nines a home is cosiest, and the cosiness is 'savoured', when a cruel or tragic event is learned of, at the safest of distances from the home (see 'Fundamental qualities' above). The 'ostrich' posture, as

177

a mechanism for the displacement of unpleasantness on to a target away from home and family, is thrown up in what the journalist went on to say: "It is far easier to think about the stranger in a white van and wish him dead, than to think of the father, the stepfather, the family 'friend', the social worker, the priest; all the people like us." Between four and nine children are murdered in the U.K. each year by strangers, and ten times as many by a family member or relative. Thousands more are abused within the home.

Newspapers do nothing to temper or educate attitudes by their headlines announcing the latest 'scare' or 'panic', and at the seamier end of the market by terms like 'monster' or 'fiend'.

Disengagement

Strain or shock, or a radical change that can not be adapted to, can cause the Nine who is not robust to disengage from normal life. Neglect is the order of the day. He is inattentive, forgetful, apathetic, even bewildered. His personal habits and dress are slovenly, and his mealtimes erratic. Long periods are spent in woolgathering. (The other type who can be slovenly is the Five.)

On being interned as a mental patient, a woman who was classed by her psychiatrist as 'delicate' and 'feeble' in constitution talked nonsense and muttered to herself. For hours on end she would lie on the floor or sit in a secluded corner. She had lost the sense of who she was, and imagined herself to be a horse, a cat, or some strange animal. One day while doing needlework she gazed at her hand, noticed a scar behind her thumb, and said, "Now I know it's me, sure enough!"

Disintegration to the Six

Integration and disintegration have thus far only been touched on here and there. They are a specialized branch of the subject, and an appendix is provided for guidance in their interpretation. Disintegration by the Nine can be so bizarre that it is worth analysis, to show how virtually any trait may be made sense of if probed for its psychological substance.

Gordon Kahl was a farmer in North Dakota who in the 1970s was the local leader of an anti-government fraternity which held that federal taxes were financing the intended destruction of Christianity by a Jewish/Communist-run banking system. Having paid no taxes for nine years he was taken to court, where he declared, "All a Christian has to know is that the income tax is the second plank of the Communist Manifesto. You can't support Satan and call yourself a Christian." When sentenced to a year in gaol he responded, "I have no choice. It's either that or an eternity in the Lake of Fire." He transferred his farm into the name of 'Gospel Doctrine Church of Jesus Christ, Alter Ego of Gordon Kahl', to prevent its seizure by the Internal Revenue Service; the ploy failed. After his release he spoke at public meetings and was interviewed, urging his fellow citizens not to pay their taxes. A T-shirt was printed bearing the legend 'Gordon Kahl is my tax consultant.' He died in a shoot-out with the police.

He went along with the crankiest of notions (the Nine) as the rationale for non-payment of tax. In court his defence of himself was immovable, and his language eccentric and archaic (the Nine). His campaigning (the Six) was his undoing.

The office manager of a cleaning company (a profession of essential maintenance, hence of the Nine) laced the drinks of his female assistant with weedkiller. In court no motive was given by him, nor did one emerge. Relations between the two of them had been good. As a Nine whose home life may have been sparse he lived largely through his job, being often at work early and late. His interests were local history and genealogy; both have a keynote of continuity and are 'close to home' (the Nine). One year his assistant bought him some

179

sweets for his birthday, and was soon astonished to be told that she was the main beneficiary in his will. He gave her gifts of money, but at the same time sent her anonymous letters containing abusive language, and began the poisoning.

An explanation for his actions is that he had an exceptionally inert or heavy emotional nature, unused to responding to anything eventful, which the kind and simple gesture of his colleague was enough to throw into a state of shock and dysfunction. His behaviour contradicted itself (the Six).

Disintegration by the Three to the Nine may be mistaken for disintegration by the Nine. A woman who is a Three was tried for the attempted poisoning of a neighbour's daughter, and was found not guilty by reason of insanity. Some six years previously her only child, to whom she had been greatly attached, had died. Since then she had become bad-tempered and malicious, making her husband's life a misery and behaving strangely, e.g. she cut her clothes to pieces, and made up her bed in a granary; her speech was incoherent. Before the act she was downcast, spoke only when spoken to, paid no attention to what was going on around her, and scarcely ate. When imprisoned, she complained of there being black cats in her cell. She imagined that she saw her daughter, heard her voice, and momentarily embraced her. In conversation she would always lead up to her (the ruminations of the Nine).

As a Three, her motivation was revenge ("This is pay-back for the death of my daughter") – but no one had wronged her. With disintegration to the Nine she invented a target, in the process acquiring an emotional obsession over her dead offspring.

The Nine and the Two

The point is made in Enneagram literature that the Two and the Nine can be mistaken for each other. This does not owe itself to any structural resonance between them, but to a predilection in some Nines who are single for social involvement that can amount to 'taking up residence' in the daily lives of others. The mode sounds parasitic, but is not so unless overdone.

John Bodkin Adams had a prosperous practice as a doctor; he is 9-8. His nature seems to have comprised a quaint and unusual mixture of greed and compassion. He charmed his elderly women patients; he would caress their hands, comb their hair, and pray with them, as well as being prepared to attend them at all hours. In the 1950s he was tried and acquitted of the murder of a wealthy widow. A search revealed a total of £45,000 in legacies to him from 132 wills; statements testified to some having been changed in his favour. In a letter from prison he wrote that "British justice and the power of prayer will clear me in God's good time." He had a lasting gratitude towards the one newspaper to have believed him not guilty; every year, on the anniversary of the acquittal, its crime reporter would be sent the message: "Thank you for another year of my life." He died in 1983. Everyone was remembered in his own will; he left over

£400,000 to 47 beneficiaries, among them 19 women who had stood by him.

As for his greed, he may have had an emotional nature that, to compensate for having been thwarted, converted itself into material need. He was once engaged, but his mother fell out with the prospective in-laws and he did not contemplate marriage again. He had expensive tastes and a sweet tooth.

It would be reasonable to deduce that he is a Two, on the basis of his having an undue sense of entitlement for going out of his way in caring for his patients, his capacity for gratitude, and the thoughtful provisions in his will.

Miscellaneous traits

Bureaucratic in generating paperwork (9-1); to be distinguished from the officious Five

Planning applications that can become interminable, or incoherent due to absence of joined-up thinking.

Unactioned reviews

Faultfinding, grumbling Suppressed anger (9-1)

The 'anorak' type of collector As an adult: homesick

Misconceptions as to type

As a source of emotional strength, 9-8 has a specific trait which could be thought to relate to the Eight. Queen Elizabeth the Queen Mother has been described as 'steel in a velvet glove'. She was instrumental in stabilizing the monarchy, on the abdication of Edward VIII, by her strength (the Eight), dependable presence (the Nine), and conservatism (the Nine). Prince Albert, a deeply fearful man, was devastated on learning that he would be King, and could not have gone forward as he did without a shoulder far more substantial than his own to lighten the load. Her Eight subtype is quite heavy (35%).

Appendix 1

TABULATIONS OF STRUCTURAL RELATIONSHIPS WITHIN THE ENNEAGRAM

Tabulation No.1

2:   life as drama

3:   the dramatic self

4:   the Scheme of Life as drama

5:   the observer; trust in reason

6:   at a varying point on the observer/participant spectrum; the issue of trust

7:    the participant; trust in life

8:   firm in strength (momentum)

9:   firm in stability (weightedness)

1:   firm in stand (faith)

Tabulation No.2

Towards: binding influence
1:   conscience
2:   state of need
6:   line of argument

Against: productive force
7:     stimuli-driven
8:   goal-driven
3:   energy-driven

Away from: state of being
4:   focus is into the imagined world of the ideal
5:   focus is into the rational world of meaning
9:   no focus

Tabulation No.3

7:   lives in the present
4:   has intimations of a past ideal
1:   life is justified by faith

2:   dependent: involvement with others
5:   independent: self-sufficient
8:   independent: self-reliant

3:   identity is equated with worth, and validated by achievement the future
6:   commitment to a position, and resultant identity the contemporary, or the present moment
9:   identifies with that which most strongly influences him the past

Tabulation No.4

7, 2, 3: expressive, insistent, enthusiastic
corresponds to childhood
averaged orientation: Against 58%, Towards 38%,
Away from4%

4, 5, 6: assesses, observes, questions
corresponds to youth
averaged orientation: Away from 63%, Towards 29%,
Against 8%

1, 8, 9: established
corresponds to adulthood
averaged orientation: in balance

The percentages are derived from apportioning three points to each type and one to each subtype, on the basis of the subtype accounting for 25% of the total, i.e. 7-6: three points apportioned to 'Against', one to 'Towards'; 7-8: four points apportioned to 'Against', and so on.

Tabulation No.5

7: externality of trust; diversity of ways; horizontal bias
1: interiority of faith; singleness of way; vertical bias

2: influence by involvement; self and action are intermixed
8: impact; self and action are separate

3: centrality of self; influences by prominence
9: merging of self; influenced by what for him assumes
prominence

Each pair comprises polar opposites. Alternatively, 1, 2, and 3 are to the centre of a circle as 7, 8, and 9 are to its circumference. In terms of apportionment as above, each pair (but not the Four and the Six) also contains an exact reversal of the orientations.

Tabulation No.6

1:   faith, and related sense of communion
6:   commitment, and related sense of belonging

2:   draws to itself (others)
7:      drawn to life

3:   creates an impression
8:   creates an impact

4:   the timeless
9:   the unchanging

1:   the enduringness of faith
9:   the unchangingness of self and life

2:   spreads: involvement
8:   draws to itself (means)

3:   creates an impression
7:      motivated by the impression made on him

4:   the aesthetic ideal
6:   the actual, existent

In both sections of the above, the focus in types 1 to 4 is on the self, whereas types 6 to 9 are other- or life-focused.

Tabulation No.7

Primary resonances

1-9 Security stems from accountability to authority, and to what are held to be the ethical or religious laws of life.

6-5 Security stems from his informing himself, being vigilant, and eliminating imponderables; in short, from providing for the position taken.

2-1 The goodness of life, as reflected in its loving source and spiritual nurture, which are the foundation of his faith. Human nature is taken to be inherently good.

7-6 The goodness of life, as reflected in the extent and intensity of all that it is possible to experience and enjoy. Human nature is taken to be good on trust.

3-2 Achievement that is recognized by, or calls attention to itself from, the world at large.

8-7 Achievement that has impact, being widespread and diversified in its effects.

4-3 The artist who attempts a representation, not necessarily on canvas, of a plane of being more ideal, because less suffused with the mundane.

9-8 The craftsman of a kind whose skill is learned by earthy familiarity and over the passage of time.

Secondary resonances

1-2 At the active interface of the specific and the general (the Two), the sense of duty that meets needs. The dynamics of need, and the right to have it met.

9-1 At the reactive interface of the specific and the general (the Nine), the upholding of that which is fundamental. The dynamics of change and resistance thereto.

2-3   Consolidated social base, bringing his presence to bear in the appropriation of agenda on the level of social management.

8-9   Consolidated power base, by the acquisition and strengthening of means on the level of business management.

3-4   He has a freedom of action that comes from being apart from the ordinariness and crowdedness of aims in life, having more rarefied ones of his own (vertical motion).

7-8   He has a freedom of action that comes from travelling along his own route. Scale arises less from strength than from being unimpeded (horizontal motion).

4-5   Values are ideal ones, unspoiled by human defect or the fashion of the moment. When they touch on the contemporary world, it is measured against them and found wanting.

6-7   Values are those of social interdependence and the contemporary world; and of its causes, for which a stand is taken.

Notes

1-9 and 6-5 are identical in orientation, as are 4-3 and 9-8.

2-1 and 7-6 have perspectives on goodness that complement each other.

3-2 and 8-7 are almost identical in orientation, as are 3-4 and 7-8.

A correlation between 2-3 and 8-9 could be inferred from one of the names for the Eight being the Boss, whilst 2-3 can be regarded as bossy.

4-5 and 6-7 are alone in being wholly dissonant in their respective orientations.

Appendix 2

LINES OF INTEGRATION AND DISINTEGRATION

Lines of integration

1 to 7   Duty is no longer a weight but a joy, and its willing acceptance a liberation. It is undoubtedly the case that for him integration constitutes a reward for virtue: a haven reached after trials endured. As for 2 to 8 and 6 to 3, the orientations from 'Towards' to 'Against' are a process of fastening on to. For the One this means that he can relax in his faith; his striving is over.

2 to 4   This is one of the combinations that broadens the outlook, others being 1 to 4 and 6 to 9, in having the orientations from 'Towards' to 'Away from'. (The same could be said of 7 to 5, from 'Against' to 'Away from'). He is both involved (the Two) and detached (the Four); states which – in contrast to those of 4 to 2 – are compatible. He experiences approaches to and from the Greater Love of the world beyond, and is at home both domestically and in spirit.

3 to 6   In a synergy of traits, the self-belief of the Three is given a further dimension by the Six's devotion to a cause. In being identified with, his achievement transcends himself; he is of a ranking that has outgrown the competitive to embrace collective values. His experience as an achiever, or resources from his success, may feed into his sense of social responsibility or conscience.

4 to 1 Sureness and precision tighten the Four's sense of belonging in life, via the guidance of the One. This is achieved on his own terms, bypassing the contemporary in attitude, the influence of the two types converging on an interior level. Both the One and the Four are exacting towards themselves, the one in conduct, the other in aesthetic ideal; high standards of beauty and order can therefore be expected from him. Any sense of estrangement from life that he may once have felt is dissipated.

5 to 8 Autonomy is outstandingly the keynote of this combination. A self-sufficiency with no lack of means has been developed which insulates from disturbance and imposition, the Five standing above and away from the potential for them. His allegiances are to the whole and not the factional (cf. 6 to 9). In detachment (which does not mean non-participation) he may be contrasted with the stifling closeness of 8 to 5.

6 to 9 Adherence is not to one or other side on an issue but to the fundamentals, the discarding of which would bring all to naught whatever the claims as to right; in other words, to the values of unity and identity as lasting strengths. The Six has progressed to an understanding of, if not sympathy for, divergence of view. Its expression for all time is surely the words of the Apostle Paul in Galatians 3:28, "There is neither Jew nor Greek, there is neither bond nor free, there is neither male nor female: for ye are all one in Christ Jesus."

7 to 5 The world of being and of thought is discovered to be as much a part of life as is doing. An outgoing life-pattern may be relinquished, as no longer satisfying; or a restricting or disabling event may force him to look inwards for strength and strategy. The earlier state is exhausted (in the other combinations having the orientations from 'Against' to 'Away from', 3 to 9 and 8 to 5, it is the state itself that is exhausted), but by integration the Seven is reenergized.

8 to 2 Having accumulated wealth the Eight gives away a sizeable amount, either during his lifetime or posthumously. The impact is enhanced if a fund is established that is self-perpetuating. His motivation is restitutive, as in putting back for what has been taken out, or in gratitude, and not – as for e.g. the philanthropic Seven – a disposal of what is surplus to need. An example is Andrew Carnegie (8-9), who retired to devote himself to social works once he had merged his companies into the U.S. Steel Corporation. His benefactions through trusts for cultural and humanitarian purposes totalled some $450 million.

9 to 3 What was said of contentment and simplicity in chapter eleven has reference to the transition to this combination, which is characterized by ease and graduality. Not only is there an identity between the Nine and the achievement, but the latter is notable for how widely it is identified with, because embodying straightforward and decent values that could be those of anyone, together with a naturalness and lack of ego. As for 5 to 8, also with orientations from 'Away from' to 'Against', a sound foundation has been built and is capitalized on.

Lines of disintegration

1 to 4 This is one of the most abject states that exist. He is weighed down by a sense of worthlessness and separation from life as God-given, and unless counseled he may not be saved from himself. He measures his faults – and, being a One, his imagined faults – against those inherent in the human condition; a self-judgment that in its harsh unreality can bring no redemption. He shares the widened outlook of 2 to 4 and 6 to 9, in the orientations from 'Towards' to 'Away from', but only in parody.

2 to 8 If 8 to 2 is the ultimate expression of giving, 2 to 8 is the ultimate expression of need. The need that in the self-harming behaviour is evident can not be addressed, since to do so would mean the Two having to relinquish the hold that is exerted over those close at hand, who can feel that they are haplessly colluding in his regime of self-imprisonment. Clues to the state should be found in imbalanced relationships within the family.

3 to 9 The energies of the Three meet with the inertia of the Nine, locking them in a self-repeating mode of force. As for 8 to 5, the orientations from 'Against' to 'Away from' are a stalled expression that can only rework itself over the same ground like a habit. Actions may be bizarre and overdone, or beyond his control, as if he is directed to do them – which should be distinguished from the schizophrenic Six – or is a witness to them. His sexuality is often pathological.

4 to 2 Inwardly dramatic and precious in his pretensions, he is far removed from ordinary life. As for 9 to 6, in social relations he is wide of the mark – as is suggested symbolically by a negative interpretation of the orientations from 'Away from' to 'Towards'. In fact he is in the worst of all worlds, akin to being the newly arrived foreigner, not speaking the language, and next-door neighbour in one. His needs (the Two) are not understood.

5 to 7 Pleasure, even elation, accompany acts that are extravagant or violent, indicating that he is not entirely aware of the meaning of what he is doing or claiming. In some circumstances he could be mistaken for a manic Seven. Having lost his sense of detachment – the necessary distance from events negated by the Seven –, he may relate the outside world not to his ideas but to his own person, not least to his sensitivities and grievances. If he has homicidal tendencies, they are not obvious in his manner. A misconception that can here be disposed of is that he is impulsive.

6 to 3 Attitudes or beliefs that are antagonistic are adopted as a vehicle of self-aggrandizement, in compensation for his victim/loser status which is thereby obscured; but not so for his resentment, envy, and scapegoating, since they are what fuels his contempt and hatred. As for 2 to 8, the orientations from 'Towards' to 'Against' are a combination of influence and entrenchment, in a pseudo-refuge leading nowhere.

7 to 1 An analogy of the life-pattern of the disintegrated Seven is paths that are travelled along successively, each with less ease than the last, in a self-imposed limitation. He ends by feeling both shut in and shut out, and is a very high suicide risk, e.g. as a youngster who is constantly frustrated in being caught doing what is against the rules, in disintegrating he has decided that life is not worth living.

8 to 5   Control is dominant but with an inversion of itself at close quarters, in the form of mind control and the techniques of 'Big Brother'. In so far as his life revolves around the home, family members are subjected to a litany of pointless exactions or worse, their lives no longer their own. In contrast to what takes place in 5 to 8, overview is submerged in an obsession with ever-tighter control of the parts (the Five). He 'can not see the wood for the trees'.

9 to 6   As illustrated in chapter eleven, some of the most bizarre behaviour imaginable is exhibited under this combination. Actions are justified with reasoning that is naive and nonsensical, and can contradict themselves. Antagonism (the Six) – which to the healthy Nine is anathema – is conjured up out of thin air. Those who would wish to assist are taken aback at being rounded on with no motive but spite.

Appendix 3

MISCELLANEOUS TABULATIONS

Comparison of what the law represents to the One and the Six

The One	The Six
The letter of the law is served	
The law as deterrent ("Thou shalt not…"); the weight of the law, especially in 1-9	The law has two sides: wrongdoing and rights
The law as instrument for the good order of society and the enforcement of right conduct	The law as instrument for the protection of society and the regulation of its wellbeing
	The body of law governs what is permitted in matters of e.g. technical planning. This is the comfort or testing of boundaries
?The status of the defendant in law is determined by judge(s) alone	The status of the defendant in law is determined by jury (i.e. his peers: the Six) by discussion and agreement
?Sentence is fixed	Sentence may be varied by aggravating, mitigating, or exemplary factors; pleabargaining

Indulgence: deprivation polarity in the Two

Indulgence	Deprivation
Parent's love is not expressed, i.e. he/she not inclined to do so	Parent's love is deficient; Two feels unloved
Perception of failing as a parent	Perception of being failed by parent
On giving:receiving spectrum, giving function is faulty because parent's love was not received; receiving function overcompensates. Includes undue concern with being responded to in ways that affirm Two is wanted	On giving:receiving spectrum, receiving function is faulty because parent's love was not given; giving function overcompensates
Self-rewarding e.g. overeating, compulsive shopping	Self-punishing e.g. anorexic, vegetative
Assuming of blame; bad conscience	Offloading of blame; clear conscience
Precocious sexuality	Late-developing or unutilized sexuality

The content of this tabulation should be treated as tentative

Characteristics of national militarism in the Six

As exemplified by Germany (6-7) in the First World War, and by Japan (6-7) in the Second World War

The cult of the soldier
War, as the instrument that binds the nation; the army, as guardian of its wellbeing
A body of soldiers becomes a quasi-mystical comradeship, with the elimination of individuality

The exaltation of the hero
Some 5,200 Japanese gave their lives in kamikaze attacks over ten months; the first squads were formed in October 1944
Japanese reaction to the news of surrender in August 1945 was to feel disgraced (i.e. to have failed in one's duty; to have betrayed trust). To quote a Japanese broadcast, "Forgive us, 0 Emperor, our efforts were not enough. Heads bow lower and tears run unchecked." The Minister of War committed suicide
Germany's attitude to defeat in 1918 is examined in chapter eight ('Victim/loser mindset')

The psychological factor in what set Germany on her pre-1914 course towards territorial expansion – not of itself peculiar to the Six – was envy, echoing Hitler's later sentiments about the 'small size' of Germany (see 'A psychological analysis of the key themes of Hitler's *Mein Kampf*' in appendix No.4: the Six)
In Japan, an increase in the independent standing and aspirations of the military in the 1930s saw a corresponding weakening of party government (a Six scenario of competing authorities)

Appendix 4

EXAMPLES OF TYPE ANALYZED BY PERSONALITY TRAITS

George Washington

Conscientious, methodical	1, 5
The Six can also be conscientious	
Controlled, composed; wise	1, 5
In the war against the French, he experienced extreme hardship and danger	
Stout-hearted: sustained by faith or obligation =	1
Capacity to endure physical hardship =	5, 7-8
Commitment =	6
If the correlation were with the Six, the element of danger would point to the Five as subtype more than to the Seven	
Resilience =	7
As commander-in-chief of the Continental army, he was a source of hope and courage to his troops	1 (-2), 7-8
On calling a council of war, he would subordinate his own judgment to that of his generals	–
Not the Three or the Eight	
Sometimes accused of being too cautious	1, 6
Emerged from retirement out of duty	1, 6
At the Constitutional Convention, as presiding officer he harmonized disputes among the delegates	5, 7-6
As the nation's first president:	
Prudent and impartial =	1, 5
Sense of rank, occasion =	?
Declined to take sides in the war between England and France. In his Farewell Address, he stated that "The nation which indulges toward another an habitual hatred or an habitual fondness is in some degree a slave. It is a slave to its animosity or to its affection, either of which is sufficient to lead it astray from its duty and its interest"	1

In what he went on to say on this subject, he could as well have been talking of international relations in today's world, dictated as they largely are by Threes (influence) and Sixes (security): "Excessive partiality for one foreign nation and excessive dislike of another cause those whom they actuate to see danger only on one side, and serve to veil and even second the arts of influence on the other"

Conclusion: 1-2

William Wilberforce

As a young man:

Enjoyed himself; he entertained, was amusing company, and had a fine singing voice	2-3, 7-6
Tended to leave his studies until they had to be done, acquitting himself satisfactorily nonetheless	
Success without undue exertion =	3, 7
Work, as an intrusion upon pleasure =	7
Not the procrastination of the Nine, which does not have a positive result	
By his own admission, at college he was not urged to work hard or to attend lectures	
Described himself as high-spirited and fiery in his youth	7
After what he called the 'great change' in attitudes that he experienced in 1785, he would reproach himself for dissipation of time not spent in self-improvement, or over-indulgence at the meal table	1
In 1787, through contacts he induced the King to issue a renewed Proclamation for the Encouragement of Piety and Virtue, to give an impetus to the idea of the country's moral regeneration	1-2
His book A Practical View, published in 1797, advances the idea and was a best seller	
His parliamentary activity on behalf of the abolition of slavery spanned some 35 years	
To take a stand against injustice=	1, 5-6, 6
Tenacity=	6
To be undaunted in espousing a cause that not only evoked harsh opposition, but that was regarded by many as hopeless =	7-6
Hope is a cardinal virtue of the Two and the Seven	
In parliament he spoke with ease and grace	7
Sought cross-party support	7, 9
Could appear indecisive due to his desire to take the right action	1, 6
Connected with a very large number of good causes	1, 5-6

It was said of him that, by his voice and expression, "he showed that joy was the prevailing feature of his own mind, joy springing from entireness of trust in the Saviour's merits and from love to God and man"

To the poet Robert Southey there was "such a sweetness in all his   1 + 2
tones, such a benignity in all his thoughts, words, and actions
that...... you can feel nothing but love and admiration for a creature
of so happy and blessed a nature"

Conclusion: 7-6 with an admixture of 1, or 1-2 with an admixture of 7. Psychic diagnosis confirms the latter. There is a resonance between the Two and the Seven, which together far outweigh the One in strength, the One and the Two each amounting to about 35%, and the Seven to about 30%. In his younger days the influence of the One was submerged; and in having components of the One and the Seven, he succeeded in reconciling polar opposites (see tabulations Nos. 4, 5 and 7 in appendix No.1).

Thomas Clarkson is judged by some to have been the driving force behind the abolition campaign, having guided it from beginning to end; he is 5-6. He first met Wilberforce in 1787, and presented him with a copy of his Essay on the Slavery and Commerce of the Human Species.

One of the earliest pamphlets on the subject was Thoughts on Slavery by John Wesley (q.v.: the Five) in 1774. He and Wilberforce met for the only time in 1789.

Mahatma Gandhi

Learned to do what he was told	
Obedient =	1, 6
Anxious to please =	2, 6
As a youth, reserved	1, 5, 6 (-5)
Went through a phase of adolescent rebellion	6, 7
Notwithstanding the above, he was intent on moral self-improve-ment	1
The racial humiliations that he met with in South Africa awakened in him a sense of injustice, and led him to campaign on behalf of the Indian community	
Justice:	
As a universal right =	1
Through the remedying of ignorance by the spreading of knowledge =	5 (-6)
As equality of rights =	6
Advocated passive resistance	
Forbearance =	1, 5
To refuse to move, as if a dead weight =	9
Argued that it was the duty of Indians to side with the British in the defence of Natal in the Boer War, so serving their oppressors. He recruited soldiers for the British during the Great War	
To do what one judges to be ethically right, regardless of personal stand =	1
Practiced equability towards any circumstance	
Self-control =	1
Moderation =	1, 5
Detachment =	5
Non-possessive	1, 5
His sympathies were with the destitute and uneducated	1 + 2, 5-6
Studied comparative religion	1 (-9), 5-6

Conclusion: 1-9

Desmond Tutu

Obtained a Master's degree in theology	1 (-9), 5
Has an unbounded capacity for love, joy, exhilaration, delight	2
This trait finds its expression mainly in personal contact, caring, and kindness	
In performing, the correlation would be with the Two or the Seven	
His sense of humour is famously animated, even comical, and has been described as "a spilling over of goodwill"	2, 7
Has used humour to lighten or defuse situations	7-6
Passionate, emotional	
Emotionality can be associated with the Two or the Six	
To be passionate requires a specific temperament. This is not a function of the Enneagram	
It has been said that he "makes no secret of his wish to be loved", and "his own need for affirmation is mirrored in his ability to affirm others"	2
For a parishioner in the Surrey village where he lived in the 1960s, "He just loved everybody; you can't help responding to that"	
In this context, his sensitivity to lack of the acknowledging gesture, and to having his integrity questioned, may be noted	
In 1976 he wrote to Prime Minister John Vorster, appealing to his sympathies as a family man acquainted with happiness and sadness through those close to him	2
Defended his stand against apartheid with theological authority	1, 5
In a speech in the mid-1980s, he told his audience that "If Christ returned to South Africa today he would almost certainly be detained under the present security laws, because of his concern for the poor, the hungry and the oppressed"	1 (-2)

Conclusion: 1-2, the subtype being heavy.

Elizabeth Taylor

Of the temperamental first horse that she took to riding, she protested, "But he loves me. He wouldn't hurt me. You don't have to worry about King when you get on his back.…I think that he likes to know that I leave it to him – that he's the boss, and I trust him"	2, 6, 7
In Jungian terms, trust with a feeling content would be expected to relate to the Two or the Six; and with a sensation content, to the Six or the Seven	
It has been remarked of her that in her teens "She was never consumed by ambition for herself, only by an overwhelming desire to please her mother"	2, 6
Or as her mother put it, "We always seem to agree on everything"	
As an actress she admitted to having no technique, and would not give of her best until filming for real	?
A contrast with James Stewart (q.v.: the Nine)	
When bored and annoyed by the undemonstrativeness and staid habits of her second husband, Michael Wilding, she would provoke a dramatic scene which would be played out as if in a film	2
Not content to be without a partner	2
Acquisitive; lifestyle of excess	2-3, 3, 7
Richard Burton is 7-6. He may not have been joking when he said that "Half the fun of being an actor is getting away from your own disgusting self' (see 'Evasion and escapism' in chapter nine)	
Prominent in campaigning for enlightened attitudes to AIDS, many of her friends having died from the disease	2, 6

Conclusion: 2-3

Diana, Princess of Wales

As a child, she felt unwanted. "I was the girl who was supposed to be a boy"	2
Lively nature	2, 6-7, 7
Enjoyed dancing and swimming	2, 7
Helpful, caring	2, 6-7
Worked at a kindergarten	2, 7, 9
Her view of marriage was romanticized	2-3, 7
At about the time of her marriage, she became bulimic	–
The drama of the disorder points emotionally to the Two, and in physical sensation to the Seven; the warped sense of entitlement, to the Two; and the wastefulness – food being ingested only to be ejected – to the Seven. (Anorexia could have as much to do with peer group awareness and the (mis)perception of difference (the Six), hence with 6-7 and 7-6)	
Relevant to the context of drama would have been the momentous elevation of her new position	
Emotionally needy; she resented Charles' absences, and sought friends and company which would compensate	2, 6
Her state was portrayed as one of emotional victimhood	2
Manipulated the media. Her televised interview in 1995 was an emotional intrigue, its reasonableness notwithstanding	2-3
Excelled in intimate contact with the sick, homeless, dying	2-1

Conclusion: 2-3
See also 'Sense of entitlement' in chapter four

Christopher Columbus

His self-belief was absolute	3, 8
Is said to have been charming and dignified, but also autocratic and remote	–
Dignity is not a trait of the Enneagram; the other three are not incompatible with his subtype as assessed. The remoteness (the Four) may have been compounded by disdain (the Three)	
His signature is a form of emblem, self-proclaiming and ornate	3-4
On being granted royal patronage to undertake his first voyage, he felt a sense of exalted destiny in his mission to convert the natives	
Epic dimension =	3-4
Sense of mission =	5-4
Claimed for himself the first sighting of land on this voyage, whereas it was made from one of the other two vessels	
To credit oneself with another's achievement =	3
Despite the missionary zeal, the voyages had less lofty motives as well, among them the promise of riches	
Mixed motives in achievement =	3
The enticing image of Hispaniola that he portrayed to prospective colonists misrepresented conditions on the island, which were hostile and arduous	
To over-accentuate the positive =	3, 7
Given the investment in them, and that their outcome was unknowable, the voyages were a gamble for vast stakes	3-4, 8-7
In his last years, he made insistent attempts to vindicate himself. His motivation would seem to have been pride and humiliation (the Three)	
Forced the facts in order to present himself in the best light. His biographer Felipe Fernandez-Armesto, while conceding his "unequalled record of achievement", warns of "the promotional or exculpatory purposes that distorted almost every thought Columbus ever confided to paper"	3

Conclusion: 3-4

Napoleon I: his rise to power

Ambitious, proud, industrious	3, 8
Of his nature he would later reveal that "my ambition is so closely bound to my being that they are both one and the same." The correlation is thus with the Three	
Despised privilege of the kind that secures advancement	
As the attitude of the self-made man of action =	3
At college he excelled in mathematics	5
Did not succeed in allying himself with the governor of Corsica, Pasquale Paoli, whom he regarded as a hero. Paoli distrusted him, sensing – to quote Harold T. Parker – "the challenge and ambition of a self-assertive love of self"	3
As commander of the French forces in Italy in 1796, he promised his troops that "rich provinces and great towns will be in your power, and in them you will find honour, glory, and wealth"	3
The Italian campaigns were characterized by speed, surprise, daring, and improvisation	3 (-4), 7
In warfare he was attentive to logistics and skilled in map reading	5
It is said that force was the only language he understood, as exemplified in his military tactic of concentrating cannon power	3
Of the victory at Lodi he commented that "From that moment, I foresaw what I might be. Already I felt the earth flee from beneath me, as if I were being carried into the sky"	3-4

Conclusion: Three with or without a Four subtype, and with an admixture of the Five. Psychic diagnosis confirms that there is no subtype or admixture. Napoleon is an object lesson in not 'judging a book by its cover': for the impact that he had, he would be assumed to be an Eight. In fact, his opportunism alone – what would he have been without the French Revolution? – marks him out as a Three.

Isambard Kingdom Brunel

The protagonist in his own magnificent drama, he did battle with the elements of earth and water, acting as if his genius and daring would confer immunity from mishap. He twice nearly drowned, first in the construction of the Thames Tunnel, then in the aftermath of a fire on board the *SS Great Western* on her maiden voyage	3-4
Almost incapable of delegating authority; as was remarked of him, "He fancied that no one could do anything but himself." Of Robert Stephenson, he wrote that "he is decidedly the only man in the profession whom I feel disposed to meet as my equal or superior."	
His secret journal alludes to his 'self-conceit' and 'love of glory'	3
Love of glory points to 3-4	
His cost estimates were often exceeded	3, 7
Where required, imaginative inducements were proposed to land-owners to permit a railway to cross their property	
Persuasive =	3
Resourceful =	7
Drove himself excessively	3, 8
High-handed, condescending, self-justifying/excusing	3-4
The first-named trait is also one of 5-4	
Impatient	3, 7
Grandeur and elegance appealed to him	3-4
Elegance is a trait of the Four, but grandeur is not. Flowery and verbose writing style	3-4

Conclusion: 3-4

Joseph Goebbels

After graduation he encountered repeated rejection in seeking employment, and fell prey to self-pity	3
The sentiment is one of indignation ("They don't recognize my worth"), not of victimhood (the Six)	
Envious of the able-bodied, due to his club foot	3, 6
Unrestrained sexuality	3, 7
There is an overwrought quality to his diary entries detailing his impressions of, and capitulation to, Hitler	2, 7
The episode did in fact cause him the greatest emotional upheaval; he had written shortly before that "We stand at Russia's side as equal partners in the fight for freedom"	
Created the *führer* myth: Hitler as heaven-sent saviour of the German nation	3-4
Not the Seven as megalomaniac: he did not mythologize himself	
His propagandistic strategy was one of audacity, the sensational, and the stage-managed	3 (-4)
Unrivalled in his contempt for those whom he targeted	3
Conversely, he was sensitive to being humiliated himself	
Would adjust his attitude on a matter to accord with what he understood Hitler's own to be, his zeal sometimes resulting in over-compliance	
(Over-)compliance =	2, 6
Overkill (see item five above) =	3
As the war turned in the Allies' favour, he alone among the leadership worked unceasingly to combat defeatism	–
Not the Six, as the communal element is missing. The trait would seem to be related to item five above: the *führer* myth could not be disavowed, nor could his loyalty to Hitler	

Conclusion: 3-4. Psychic diagnosis confirms that there is no subtype.
Item four above suggests 3-2, but it is pertinent to state that his extraordinary reaction to Hitler had no parallel in his relationships with women.

John F. Kennedy

Confided to a friend, "My mother was either at some Paris fashion house or else on her knees in some church. She was never there when we really needed her… My mother never really held me and hugged me"	2
In his naval service in the Second World War, he was both courageous and negligent	–
The strength of motivation in someone having this combination of traits is open to question	
Charming, energetic	3, 7
Unrestrained sexuality	3, 7
His presidency carried the sense of a nation reborn, and reinspired to greatness	3-4
As President, his approach was direct – rather than through meetings and committees – and as head of a team. His objectives were what would yield results in the short term	3
The forthrightness of his speeches contrasts with the hesitancy and half-heartedness of many of his actions on the domestic front	–
This trait is explained less by natural caution than by expediency (the Three): powerful interest groups could not be alienated	
In the Bay of Pigs fiasco, his desire to be seen to act outweighed the evaluation of what was being proposed	–
See next item	
Before the meeting with Khrushchev in 1961 he said, "I have to show him that we can be just as tough as he is"	3, 6
Charges of being 'soft' on Communism had to be avoided	
Khrushchev is 5-6, and can be classed as a reformer (destalinization, 'peaceful coexistence'). The subtype is heavy, which is the reason for his sometimes blustering manner	
A gulf of misrepresentation (distortion, exaggeration, omission) was created between the image – the appearance of sincerity and conviction – and the reality	3

Conclusion: 3-2
U.S.A. is also 3-2.

Jim Jones

A friend of his from early days recalled, "I had been to Jim's house to have supper with him, and I said, "I've got to go home." Jim said, "Don't leave", and he was very forceful... He reached over and he grabbed that pistol and he let the first one go, and so I turned, and then I really started running, and he fired again... It didn't hit me.... That's the last time I ever went to his house"

Outrage at losing attention ("I am worth your being with. How dare you leave me until I say so!") =	3 (-4)

An astonishingly charismatic evangelist who preached a messianic socialism, in the 1950s he founded the People's Temple in the U.S., a church integrating white and black, rich and poor, and which was commended for its social projects. He was voted San Francisco's Humanitarian of the Year in 1977   3-4

According to one witness, "If you would watch him, and listen to him, he had you, and he knew that." For another, "He had a method of penetrating your mind with his eyes, and he could control you"

In church he was alleged to have spit on, and stamped on, the Bible

Sacrilege =	3-4
The hoped-for 'Promised Land' in Guyana was a labour camp ruled by fear: an escape to nowhere	?7-8 to 1

On 18th November 1978, in the course of his harangue whilst the mass suicide/murder which claimed 913 lives was taking place, he said, "I've never lied to you. I'm the best friend you'll ever have. You'll regret it if you don't die"

To betray, by persuasion and abandonment =	3

It was not in his plan that he himself would die

Conclusion: 3-4
He is described as having become "a part of his own paranoia", but that was not quite his state. He had no fear for himself – wrongly, as it transpired, since he was shot in the mayhem of the last hours. As a Three, what he did have was a determination to retain his hold over his one-time devotees (see item two above).

Madonna

As a youngster:

Attention-seeking	2-3, 6 + 7
Self-driven; high achiever	3
Defiant: she did not like being told what to do, and would wear her clothes as she wished	6, 7-6
Learned how to shock	6-7
What brought her to the notice of those who promoted her was her physical presence, energy, and aggressive confidence	3, 7

In the formative years of her career:

Any kind of relationship was a means of advancement, to be discarded once some mileage had been gained from it	3
As she has said, "You take what you can and then move on" Not with the Two: her behaviour was not adapted to, or shaped by, the interpersonal; nor a tactic of the Seven who values contacts made, since bad feeling could result	
Regarded admitting to need as a weakness	3, 6
To the Three, the admission is humiliating and a failing; to the Six, it is taking a risk by letting go of a defence (i.e. the appearance of strength)	
Impatient	3, 7
Outspoken and argumentative	6
Ambivalent towards religion, and disrespecting of its imagery	6
Her disrespect was meant to shock, not an expression of contempt (the Three)	

Her book *Sex*, published in 1992, was:

An over-hyped piece of self-marketing	3
Controversial: in developing her career, she consistently 'crossed the line' in setting new boundaries	6
As an artist, she has kept pace with contemporary trends in music and dance	6

Conclusion: Three with no subtype, and an admixture of the Six

213

Ludwig van Beethoven

His attitude towards being plagiarized was robust. In a letter to Eleonore von Breuning he refers to "those Viennese pianists, some of whom are my sworn enemies"	6, 8
Could be suspicious of others' motivation	6

Having had a friendly meeting with him in 1812, Goethe writes of him as being "an utterly untamed personality, who is not altogether in the wrong in holding the world to be detestable but surely does not make it any the more enjoyable either for himself or for others by his attitude"

To be out of sympathy with life =	4

Until he secured publishers for his music he was dependent on the aristocracy for subsidy, but was no respecter of their conventions; they were obliged to indulge him

To be a stranger to conformity =	4, 5-4
To take a position by not conforming =	6
Had a capacity for sustained withdrawal into the mind	5

It is recounted that he could sit for hours sunk in thought in a restaurant, and then offer to pay for a meal that he had not eaten

Resolute that his deafness would not handicap him as a composer	8

In social commitment, the correlation would be with the Six; and in the desire not to forgo, with the Seven

A diary entry of about 1813 states that "for thee there is no longer happiness except in thyself, in thy art"	4-3
His music is without equal in its intensity, striving, and range of expression	4 + 8

Conclusion: 8-7 with an admixture of 4. Psychic diagnosis confirms 4-3 with admixture of 8.

Franz Schubert

In his eighteenth year he composed almost 150 songs, in addition to his output of string quartets, symphonies, and masses   7

This was at a time when he was teaching at his father's school, attending concerts and operas, and taking lessons in composition! In 1824 he coached the two daughters of Countess Esterhazy for some months. One day at breakfast she invited him to set to music for their four voices a poem of which she was fond. He "took the book and retired immediately in order to compose. In the evening of the same day we were already trying through the finished song at the piano from the manuscript"

His compositions are rich in the representation of imagery through melody and technical effect (e.g. the 'Trout' Quintet)   4-3

The counterpart in literature is 5-4

Fused classical form with art-song (*lieder*)   7

See 'Extension and connection' in chapter nine

Drawn to the work of poets, to the text of which he would set his songs   –

See item two above

Moods of resignation and despair intermittently descended on him   4, 6

During his first sojourn on the Esterhazy estate in 1818, he wrote to some friends, "Thank God I live at last." His elation was soon to evaporate

Disliked being flattered   1, 4

If the sentiment were distrust instead of dislike, the correlation would be with the Six

Thirty years after his death, it was written of him that he had a dual nature, "the Viennese gaiety being interwoven and ennobled by a trait of deep melancholy. Inwardly a poet and outwardly a kind of hedonist"   4 + 7

Conclusion: 4-3 with an admixture of 7. The admixture would have mitigated his depression and any sense of estrangement (the Four).

Vincent van Gogh

As a youngster, serious, aloof, morose, self-conscious	4, 5-4
In England he had a fantasized love affair, which ended on his learning that the girl was engaged to be married	
To idealize womanhood (the ideal is not accessible) =	4
To fantasize because it is 'safe' =	6
Not an infatuation (typically the Two or the Seven), which would not have ended at that point	
After this crisis he embraced "the worship of sorrow", declaring that "sorrow is better than joy"	
Perspective conditioned by capacity for sadness =	4
Self-tormenting, self-accusing	1, 4
Fame was, to him, a snare	–
Those who are famous, but who insist on a life of seclusion, are in this category; most are 5-4	
The bleak and oppressed images that as artist he favoured, in nature and man, were for him truth and beauty	4
Worked in a coalmining area of Belgium as an evangelist, social worker, and teacher	1 + 2, 5
Maintained a vast correspondence with his brother Theo	5, 7
Frustrated by satisfaction being beyond his reach, whether in art or relationships	4

Conclusion: 4-3 with an admixture of 5

King Alfred ('The Great') of Wessex

Sought to revive literacy and learning in his kingdom, assembling scholars from all quarters at his court, and translating religious and classical texts into English. He wrote that "I can not find anything better in man than that he know, and nothing worse than that he be ignorant"

Philosophical or ethical teachings =	1 (-9), 5
Acquisition of knowledge =	5
Relied upon authoritative texts, his thinking being derivative, not original	1, 6

To his translation of a work by Boethius is appended a prayer of his own: "Lord God Almighty, confirm me against the devil's temptations; and keep far from me foul lust and all iniquity....... that I may inwardly love You before all things with pure thought and clean body"

Desire for moral self-improvement =	1
Fear of temptation =	1
Concern with personal purity, cleanness =	1, 5
Practical, inventive	5-6, 7
His first dealings with Viking marauders were governed by pragmatism	5-6

7-6 would be a secondary correlation to this trait, were it not for his lack of trust towards them due to their propensity for treachery and, most significantly to him, for oath-breaking

After victory over the Vikings in 878, their king Guthrum was baptized and feted at his court, and became his adoptive son or godson. His intention was to bind Guthrum and his nobles to himself in a secure community of interests	6

For future defence against Viking invasion, to replace a levy of king's men he instituted a standing army, one half of which would guard the home lands whilst the other half waged war, the two in rotating contingents; and a network of garrisoned fortresses

Defensive measures =	6

Conclusion: 5-6
In general this subtype is more suited to leadership than 5-4, because more in touch with the contemporary world (the Six).

Isaac Newton

As a youngster he was always in thought, much taken with mechanical models and contrivances, and socially perverse   5

At university, "thinking all hours lost, that was not spent in his studies", he rarely dined in the hall, and when he did the meal could be cleared away before he had eaten anything; he was a very neglectful host when having friends to entertain, which was seldom; he took no recreation, and was careless in his dress   5

Obviously not the self-abstraction of the Nine, which shows itself in woolgathering, or 'wandering off somewhere'

Until he adopted more rounded habits in later years, he avoided company and discouraged correspondence   5-4

Academically hypersensitive; wary of making his findings known   5

Detested argument   –

See preceding three items

Discovered the infinitesimal calculus   5

Investigated the theoretical composition of light   5-4

Formulated the Jaw of universal gravitation, and speculated on the causative substance of motion   5-4

To experiment with moving objects would correspond to 5-6

When he felt his professional progress slowing or his standing threatened, he could be domineering and petty, even vindictive, as demonstrated by the shameful episode of F1arnsteed's astronomical catalogue, of which Newton had an unauthorized version printed to suit his needs; F1amsteed secured the return to himself of the undistributed copies by court order   5

Conclusion: 5-4

John Wesley

As a student at Oxford, he began the habit of noting on paper his faults of character and their remedies

Self-examination =	1, 5

In the case of the Five, self-analysis might be a better word

Urged 'method and order' on his colleagues in Christian studies and practice, so that each hour of the day had its proper use

As a moral duty =	1
For productive efficacy =	5

In February 1738 he met Peter Bohler, a Moravian brother. In discussing with him and seeking his counsel over the next three months, Wesley came over to the belief that salvation is by faith: a gift to the believer which may be availed of at any instant and not – as he had been preaching – a reward dispensed at last to the earnest in striving and good works   5, 6

His openness of mind points to the Five, as does his hope that the Methodists would be a society of Christians and not a denomination

Addressed himself to the poor	1 +2, 5-6

It is said that he "wore his learning so lightly that the simplest hearer could understand"   ?5-6

cf. William Tyndale in chapter seven

When faced with what he could not decide upon, he sometimes wrote down the choices and drew a lot

Randomness =	5
His literary output was vast and varied, some of it classical in origin	5 (-4)
Itinerant: not domiciled in his own parish. As was inscribed on his memorial: "I look upon all the world as my parish"	5

A contrast with the Nine

Conclusion: 5-6. Psychic diagnosis confirms that there is no subtype; as such, it could be said that his religion was more sought after than prescribed (the Six). In any walk of life, the Five with no subtype is without bias towards the ideal (the Four) or the actual/existent (the Six) (see tabulation No.6 in appendix No.1).

Jean-Jacques Rousseau

The dominant theme of his works is the innocence of man corrupted: the ideal lost to the sophisticated and civilized	4

See 'Inappropriateness to life' in chapter six

Made a case, in disputing with the composer Jean-Philippe Rameau, for the free expression of melody to have priority over the formality of harmony	7

In his *Discourse on the Origin of Inequality*, he postulates that vice in man is not inherent but due to his social propensity, arising from the right to possess (e.g. envy), the comparison of social position (e.g. pride), and the conflict of interests

Disinclination to social interaction =	5 (-4)
His conception of justice is Platonic and mechanistic	5

See 'Other virtues' in chapter three

A contrast with justice as the relief of oppression (the One), the removal of grievance (5-6), or the claiming and exercising of rights (the Six)

Advocated a social order in which sovereignty resides in the citizens. The powers of government and representative bodies are thus derivative, in carrying out the will of the citizens

Theories concerning the ideal organization of society =	5-4

The social theorist as 5-6 would treat of society as it is

Information was to be freely taken up, with debate and decision not affected by any factional interest. As he wrote, "Each citizen should think only his own thoughts"	5
His approach to religion was mystical and minimalist	5

Conclusion: 5-4

Thomas Jefferson

Conscientious and meticulous	1, 5
Observant, inventive	5, 7
Inclined to moderation of expression	1, 5
Acquired a knowledge of French and classical languages, to which were later added Spanish, Italian, and Anglo-Saxon	5, 7
Had a lifelong interest in:	
Natural science, social philosophy, literature	5 (-6)
Architecture; he designed the University of Virginia and supervised its construction	?
The one example of an architect that I have is Albert Speer, who is in fact 5-6	
In the 1770s he was at the forefront in defending the rights of British America, arguing that the British Parliament had no authority to legislate for the colonies	5-6, 6
Took the predominant part in the framing of the Declaration of Independence	?1, 5
Engaged in law reform	1, 5-6
Desired an educational system that would provide universal literacy, and informed views through a free press. As he vowed, "I have sworn upon the altar of God eternal hostility against every form of tyranny over the mind of man"	5
As Minister to France, and witness to the suppression of liberties, he realized that the question of rights could not be left as self-evident but must be specified. To that end, he was instrumental in procuring the Bill of Rights	
Combination of foresight and safeguard =	5 + 6
Considerations of security and stability governed his thinking in proceeding with the purchase of the Louisiana Territory	6

Conclusion: 5-6

Charles Dickens

Acutely observant; mastery of written language	5
Drawn in his imagination to the dark side of life: misery, decay, the mysterious, the gruesome	?
In the reaction evoked, that which is decaying or gruesome relates to the Six	
Describes his characters in detail by the clothes that they wear	
In so far as this is to connect appearance with social standing or respect =	6, ?9
A smart dresser himself, which is often a trait of the Seven. Orphans, and the sympathy that they arouse, are a constant feature of his novels	6
Depicts characters whom he knew	5 (-4)
Satirist, whose wit could be razor-sharp	6
Could be very excitable, emotional, extravagant in manner, impulsive, restless	7
It can be speculated that he may have had a fourth ray emotional nature, in terms of Alice Bailey's teachings on the Seven Rays, which would be quite unusual for a Five	
In moods of despondency he had a sense "as of one happiness I have missed in life, and one friend and companion I have never made" Devastated by the death at the age of seventeen of Mary Hogarth, his wife Catherine's sister, of whom he said, "She had not a single fault"	4
Overworked himself	–
Financial security could have been a factor: when he was twelve, his father was imprisoned as a debtor, and Charles was sent to work in a blacking warehouse	
Actor, entertainer	6-7, 7, 9
In later years he gave dramatic readings from his works, and seems to have needed the admiration (the Six)	
Concerned with welfare issues	1, 5

Conclusion: 5-6 with an admixture of 4. Psychic diagnosis confirms that there is no admixture of the Four (nor of the Seven).

David Livingstone

Studied theology, medicine, chemistry, and Greek	5
Languages which are of the past or obscure suggest 5-4	
Self-sufficient	5
Plain-spoken, curt; he could antagonize without being aware of it Declared that "I would never build on another man's foundations"	4
Compiled a Setswana dictionary	5 (-4), 7
On his trans-African journey begun in 1853, he charted his course meticulously	5
Recorded all that he observed and encountered in a journal covering eight hundred pages	5, 7
Felt that he had been designated by God in his mission to open up the land to commerce, which he envisaged would relieve poverty and displace slavery. His mood could be exalted	3-4, 5-4
Endured the greatest hardships, and was fearless	–
See item above	
In *Missionary Travels* he omitted details of whatever could deter commercial interest in the area	–
See item eight above	
His ability to work harmoniously with colleagues was very limited. On the Zambezi Expedition his conduct towards them was accusatory and petty	–
See items two, three, and eight above	
Unfortunately he needed them	

Conclusion: 5-4
Much is made of his supposed hypomania, but this diagnosis overlooks the fact
that the symptoms stemmed from his thoughts and not his actions.

Gregor Mendel

A natural scientist, his favoured subjects of study were botany and meteorology	5 (-6)
Modest; not overly confident	1, 5, 6
Ordained as a priest in 1847, it was soon realized that he was unsuited to his parish duties as he could hardly bring himself to minister to the sick and dying. The abbot of his monastery in Brno reported that Mendel was "seized by an unconquerable timidity when he has to visit a sick-bed." Instead he taught	?5
Obviously an expression of fastidiousness, but not the standard one of the Five	
Sought to determine whether the transmission of characteristics in identical plants is constant; then, as he wrote, to "deduce the law according to which they appear in successive generations" when hybrid plants are created through cross-breeding	
To discover natural law =	5-4
Painstaking and meticulous: in one season he had to shell, count, and sort by shape more than 7000 peas – for just one experiment	5
In its entirety, his project involving the garden pea plant occupied him for eight years. His discoveries were the foundation of what became the science of genetics	

Conclusion: 5-4. Psychic diagnosis confirms 5-6; as such, his work was concerned more with systematizing what he found than with speculating on what might be.

Charles Darwin is 7-6 and not, as would be thought, 5-6.

An uncut (i.e. unread) reprint of Mendel's first journal article of 1866 was in Darwin's possession. Mendel had read On the Origin of Species in a German language edition published in 1860, annotating his copy in the margin with his observations.

Lewis Carroll

Genteel, reserved, industrious, meticulous	5
Could be precious	4
Not improved by his sheltered existence	
Mathematician	5(-4)
Satirized the administration of his Oxford college	5
Much enjoyed the company of young girls	5,7
It is rare for this trait – as in his case – not to have unsavoury associations	
Photographed young girls, clothed or nude	
In so far as this is an opting for the ideal over the real, the latter being womanhood =	4
His fairy-tales are characterized by:	
Surrealism of a kind that is dreamy, constantly shifting and trans-forming itself:	?
The theme of meaning =	5
Inverted logic:	5-4
The presence of the Four enlarges the perspective to include that which is strange, and may be contrasted with the reductionism of the known in 5-6	
Thematic trails as in literature ("I had sent my heroine straight down a rabbit-hole, to begin with, without the least idea what was to happen afterwards") =	5-4
See 'Modalities of thought' in chapter seven	
Not to be confused with improvisation by the Seven, to move things forward or to extricate himself; or by the Nine, to preserve continuity	
Perfectionist – and to those commercially involved, tediously so – in relation to his books as a finished product	4
For some forty years he kept a register summarizing letters sent and received, which by the time of his death amounted to nearly one hundred thousand items	5, 7

Conclusion: 5·4

225

Joseph Rowntree

As the Firm of Rowntree* prospered in the late 1800s, the number of its employees grew rapidly. In 1890 a new site was bought, which enabled him in due course to bring about working conditions that were healthy and pleasant. He believed that the employees' goal should be their "self-development in all that is best and most worthy." Amenities were provided which were comprehensive

In his speech marking the opening of the school in the model village of New Earswick which he pioneered, he said, "In the supreme work of building up character, the most potent influence will no doubt come from the teachers." The girls' education was to be "as liberal as that of the boys", in which respect he continued, "Sewing and cooking will not be neglected, but we want the girls when they grow up to be able to enter with intelligent understanding and sympathy into all the wider interests of men, so that they may be true and helpful companions to their husbands and able wisely to guide the minds of children"

Enlightened social and educational attitudes =   5 (-6)

When a company Pension Fund was instituted in 1906, he made a personal contribution of £10,000 towards its start-up solvency (the Firm itself contributed about £9000)

In 1917 the fund was extended to cover provision for widows   –

The most likely correlation is with the One (a measure that is ethically right), the Five (as above), or the Six (commitment)

For nearly forty years he taught every Sunday morning at the Adult   5
School (the offshoot of a school started by York Friends in 1848), and became acquainted with the abuse of alcohol in the home life of working men, on which topic he co-authored several books. His approach was factual and statistical, not moral

Conclusion: 5-6

*The 'Cocoa, Chocolate and Chicory Works' was purchased in 1862 by his younger brother Henry Isaac, and traded as H.I. Rowntree & Co. Before long Joseph joined, him as a partner; Henry died in 1883. Rowntree & Co. Ltd. was incorporated in 1897.

Eamon de Valera

At college he specialized in pure mathematics, algebra, and geometry	5-4
Taught mathematics and physics	5
Diligent, meticulous, austere, pedantic	1, 5
Took on the 'aura of the dead' after the Easter Rising of 1916, becoming the embodiment of a romanticized ideal of Irishness	
Sense of mission =	5-4
As he wrote in 1920 when campaigning in the U.S. to raise funds, via a very contentious bond issue, for the projected government, "I am answerable to the Irish people for the proper execution of the trust with which I have been charged. I am definitely responsible to them, and I alone am responsible"	
Intransigent, high-handed, given to tactical manoeuvres for his own ends	3-4, 5-4
These traits can not be divorced from the foregoing item; nor can the rewriting of the facts in his authorized biography	
Wished everything around him to be free of grounds for his suspicion	5
Controlled every aspect of the Irish Press	8
Insisted on the country's neutrality in the Second World War	
Impartiality =	1, 5
Non-involvement =	5
Avoidance of conflict =	9
His backward-looking attitudes militated against Ireland's development, whether in prosperity or international relations	4

Conclusion: 5-4

Ho Chi Minh

Shadowy, enigmatic. It is estimated that during his lifetime he adopted more than fifty pseudonyms; he even used one in writing an autobiography, in which he referred to himself in the third person	5, 6-5
Patient, cautious; very modest in his material needs	1, 5
As a teacher, he did not side either with the resistance to French administration of Indochina or with the reformists, distrusting both. He chose first to go abroad in order to understand at the source	5
The petition which he handed to delegates at the Versailles Conference in 1919 was framed largely in terms of freedoms sought ('liberté de presse', 'liberté d'association' etc.), and a fair system of justice	5, 6
In 1924, having studied in the Soviet Union for over a year he departed for China, where as a representative of the Comintern he had a liaising and developing role of training, organizing, establishing contacts, and reporting	
To organize for effective functioning =	5
To organize for growth =	7
A role having a variety of facets =	7
His methods were didactic: writing and lecturing	5
They were not based on the appeal of personality (the Three), force of argument (the Six), or the attractions of the subject (the Seven)	
Pragmatist	5
In his speech declaring the independence of Vietnam on 2nd September 1945, the opening words underlined the concepts of freedom and equality of rights	5
Flattered countries which were potential benefactors to Vietnam	–
His motive was tactical; see item seven above	
Despite being by nature a moderate, he did nothing to halt the over-zealous implementation of land reform in the mid-1950s	–
See foregoing item: China could not be alienated	

Conclusion: 5-6
Vietnam is 6-7. The decisive quality displayed by the North in the Vietnam War was defensive tenacity.
Pham Van Dong, who was prime minister of North Vietnam for 32 years, is 5-4. An austere, remote, and cultured figure, he had first met Ho Chi Minh in China in the mid-192os. Ho referred to him as 'my other self' and 'my favourite nephew.'

Bob Dylan

In his younger days he had great nervous energy, and could be impulsive	7
Whether rock and roll, blues, or folk, his tastes in music are for the authentic. The style of performance that he made his own has been called rough and raw	4
His songs tend to be poetry set to music	4-3, 5-4
Being himself a songwriter, 5-4 is the more likely	
On embarking on his career in the 1960s, his compositions tapped into the social awareness – protest, idealism – of youth	5, 6, 7
Not the Six, in his case, as he was not a campaigner rallying to a cause or taking a stand against authority	
Did not adapt his style to please the audience	
A 'take it or leave it' attitude =	5
When recording he did not communicate with band members, who had to ascertain his intentions by closely observing him	5
Enigmatic: parried questions about himself or his views; not at home in a formal interview setting	5
His relationships were numerous and capricious. Sometimes he was less than upright in how he treated a partner	
Emotionally semi-detached =	5
Changeable =	6
Casual=	7
While not abandoning Judaism, in 1979 he was baptized	5, 6, 9
Causative factors are: in the Five, a search for meaning and substance, or an emptiness of being; in the Six, a need to belong and for companionship, and a belief in the rightness of the new religion as the justification for belonging to it; and in the Nine, the over-whelming impression that the religion has made on him	

Conclusion: 5-4

Peter Sutcliffe ('The Yorkshire Ripper')

As a child, quiet and shy. He clung to his mother and the home	4-5, 5, 6-5
At school he was variously described as someone who would never refuse a 'dare' and liked to raise a laugh in the classroom, yet as not wanting to draw attention to himself or simply blushing when looked at	?4, ?5-4
A very strange disposition! Not the oscillation of the Six, since to vary from exhibitionist to inhibited can not be classed as a single behavioural range	
Did he feel that he had a specialness, which his inhibition curbed?	
Worked as a gravedigger for three years, and had a macabre sense of humour	5
Not to be confused with the Six, in whom the comparable humour has to do with thoughts and intimations of death, not with dead bodies as such	
In prison in the 1980s he painted a picture of himself and his wife (she divorced him in 1994) which is ornate, stiff in its formalism, and idealized in placing them in a genteel country setting belonging to a past age (one or two hundred years ago?)	4 + 5

Conclusion: 5-4. Psychic diagnosis reveals a relative suppression of the Five over time, so that by default the Four appears as of now to be type and not subtype. In court he stated that in 1967 he had been directed to kill prostitutes, which was not accepted as his motivation. Nonetheless, to have a pathological sense of mission is a trait of 5-4; examples are David Icke, Timothy McVeigh, and Eric Harris, ringleader of the Columbine High School massacre. (Icke once proclaimed himself 'the spirit of the Son of God', sent to prevent mankind from destroying itself in 1997; McVeigh bombed the Murrah federal building in Oklahoma City "to put a check on government abuse of power where others have failed"; in a note left by Harris he wrote, "If you are reading this, my mission is complete").

In 1969 he had picked up a prostitute and given her the money, but was unable to go further. Three weeks later he saw her in a pub and demanded his money back, whereupon she recounted the incident so that the other customers would hear, making him a laughing-stock. Being hypersensitive, he would have internalized the experience, reinforcing the impulse that he claimed already to have.

Aung San Suu Kyi

At college in the U.K. she studied philosophy, politics, and economics	5
Strong personal morality; temperate	1, 5
Dry humour	5
Took up the legacy of her father's struggle*	
Sense of mission =	5-4

In 1998 she attempted four times to visit NLD party members outside Rangoon, where she lived, and was prevented from continuing her journey by road-blocks set up by the ruling junta. On one occasion she was returned to her home by security forces after a six-day protest in her car. In another incident she was returned by ambulance, having spent 13 days in the car

See item above

Kept herself occupied in confinement by studying, exercising, meditating, practicing her French and Japanese, and playing Bach on the piano   5-4

Conclusion: 5-4

*The National League for Democracy, which she co-founded in 1988, won the last general election in Burma in 1990, gaining 60% of the votes. The result was not recognized by the junta, which had already placed her under house arrest. Released in 1995 but under periodic restrictions, she was rearrested in 2000 and again released in 2002.

In March 1999 the junta refused to grant a visa to her husband, Michael Aris, who was dying from cancer, and encouraged her to visit him in the U.K., which she declined to do for fear that she would not be permitted to return. Her husband died later that month.

Her father, Aung San, was one of the '30 comrades' who liberated Burma from foreign rule, and was assassinated in 1947 when she was two.

King Charles I

Conscious of a lack of affection and family contact. In his earliest years, his care was entrusted to others; his brother and sister were gone from his life by the time he was twelve

Sense of abandonment =	6
Had wished to emulate his brother	6

Emulation is a comparative trait

Keen to please his father	1, 2, 6
Observed a conscientious routine in his duties as king	1, 5, 6
Reserved, refined, fastidious	5 (-4)

Could be dogmatic or indecisive

To contradict oneself =	6

Would agree with his advisers and later change his mind, not consult them, or take advice in secret from elsewhere

His dogmatism was a mask for indecisiveness

Devious, capable of breaking his word, even of disloyalty

For personal gain, or in walking away from failure =	3
To safeguard one's position =	6

His own trust could be misplaced

Avid (obsessive?) collector of fine works of art

Taste for splendour =	3-4
Aesthetic sense =	3-4, 4, 5-4
Obsessive=	5

This trait is out of character with the other indications of his type, and could be a psychological compensation for emotional impoverishment

As war leader, brave yet irresolute	6

See item six above

Conclusion: 6-5

United States of America:
causative and early personality traits

From the 1760s, antagonism towards England arose from the imple-   6
mentation of measures which strengthened its administration

Perhaps the most decisive factor was the opposition of settlers and   6 + 7
land speculators to the limits on expansion imposed by the Treaty of
Paris in 1763

In the Declaration of Independence, the case is made for "the
necessity which denounces our Separation", by a listing of grievances

To make a case based on grievances =   5-6

The people were to have "the separate and equal station to which the
Laws of Nature and of Nature's God entitle them." It was deemed their
right and duty "to provide new Guards for their future security"

Entitlement to the same rights =   6

Security considerations =   6

Qualities driving the migratory movement westward were free- spir-   7
itedness, hope, resourcefulness, and resilience

In 1860, divided loyalties resurfaced (they had been present at inde-   6
pendence) with the issue of slavery, and in the next year civil war: a
conflict of impulses between traditional and contemporary/liberal
values, and secondarily between desires and conscience

See 'Conflict of impulses' in chapter eight

Conclusion: 6-7

Thomas Jefferson (q.v.) is 5-6.

The neutrality intended by George Washington (q.v.: 1-2) is not a trait of the Six
and was unsustainable.

In about 1865 the Enneagram type changed to 3-2, corresponding to the growth
by wealth-creation with which tile country is synonymous.

Abraham Lincoln

As a youth, he acquired a reputation for telling anecdotes and yarns, had a ready wit, and could mimic	6 + 7
Given to brooding, which could deteriorate into depression	4, 6
Practiced as a lawyer	1, 6

This does not take account of those for whom the profession could constitute a stage for self-expression e.g. the Three

In his first campaign address in 1832, he wrote of the nature of his ambition: "I have no other so great as that of being truly esteemed of my fellow men, by rendering myself worthy of their esteem"

Desire to be well regarded or looked up to =	6

Uppermost in his mind at that time was what he could cause to be done by way of economic measures which would bring local benefit

His views on the abolition of slavery were:

Ethical, reasoned =	1, 5 (-6)
Dictated by duty; respecting of the law as it stood =	1, 6
Broad-based; avoiding of the sectional =	7, 9
Conservative, gradualist =	9

In 1845 he wrote that it was "a paramount duty of us in the free states, due to the Union of the states, and perhaps to liberty itself (paradox though it may seem) to let the slavery of the other states alone", and that "we should never knowingly lend ourselves… to prevent that slavery from dying a natural death – to find new places for it to live in, when it can no longer exist in the old"

Despite considering slavery to be an injustice ("my oft-expressed personal wish that all men every where could be free"), as he declared in 1862, "My paramount object in this struggle is to save the Union, and is not either to save or to destroy slavery"

To stand above what is in contention (the Six), in seeking a resolution that preserves the fundamentals (the Nine) =	6 to 9

As President, he assembled a diverse cabinet

Diversity of interests =	7
Alternatively, in so far as the preceding item is relevant =	9
Cautious; patient; pondered matters with care and at length before arriving at a judgment, consulting and listening to advice	1, 6

At the ceremony for his second inauguration in March 1865, the tone of his address was marked by:

Communal commitment =	6
Conciliation =	6 to 9, 7

This was not a blanket peaceableness (the Nine), but the sentiments of someone who could see – even sympathize with – the reasons for dissenting positions

Exemplary for his strength of character and devotion to duty	1, 6

Conclusion: 6-7 integrated to 9. According to psychic diagnosis, he began integrating in about 1838.

Alice A. Bailey's The Externalisation of the Hierarchy contains a reference to him under the heading 'Racial Avatars' (p.298; Christopher Columbus (q.v.: the Three) is earlier mentioned also).

General Gordon

In the Crimean War as an engineer, he thrived in the rough   –
conditions and found military action exciting, sometimes courting
danger with a kind of fatalism. He was thorough in carrying out
reconnaissance

Those to whom physical comfort matters least are Fives. The
combination of excitement and danger is one of the Seven and the Six
respectively. Fatalism is mostly a trait of the Six. To reconnoitre is to
establish how best to proceed (the Five), or whether the area is safe
(the Six)

In 1859 he was appointed to the expeditionary force in China, and   1,
became commander of the 'Ever Victorious Army' which suppressed   5-6,
the Taiping rebels. In leadership he was fearless, practical, respected,   6, 7
and unassuming

Gave tactical consideration in warfare to ways in which, from case to   –
case, the enemy could be weakened

"I am strengthened by that which weakens my enemy" is a mindset of
relativity, hence of the Six

Possibly connected with reconnaissance: see note to item one above,
on the Five

On the fall of Soochow to Gordon's army the governor of Shanghai
province promised him that the lives of the rebel leaders would be
spared. In the event he received them and then departed, whereupon
they were massacred by his troops. Gordon was distraught at his
treachery, and at himself for having trusted him. His first impulse
was to write a letter (which was unsent) demanding the governor's
resignation; if that were not forthcoming, Gordon would recapture
the towns that he had taken from the rebels and, as a mark of
penitence, restore them to their control. The governor attempted to
make peace with him, acknowledging responsibility for the massacre,
and sending him gifts on behalf of the Emperor, for which Gordon
thanked his Highness but which he declined to accept

Issues of treachery, conscience, (self-) forgiveness   6

Returning to England in 1865, he wanted nothing of the fame that   5
the country wished to bestow on him, nor even to associate with
mainstream society. He destroyed the journal of his operations in
China

While at Gravesend, as Chief Royal Engineer supervising the   5
construction of a series of forts along the Thames, he took into his
home young boys who were waifs. He fed and clothed them at his
own expense, taught them in the evenings, and found them jobs
when they were old enough

Compare with Thomas Barnardo (q.v.: the Seven)

Leisure time at Gravesend was spent visiting the sick and dying,   5
comforting them with Bible readings and conversation

Tireless in his commitment to sound administration, first as governor   5-6,
of Egypt's equatorial provinces, then as governor-general of the entire   6
Sudan

Waiting for Khartoum to be overrun by the Mahdi's forces, he passed   1, 6
his last days in January 1885 in a brooding and confessional frame of
mind, as revealed by his journal

Restless and impatient by nature, as if there were no time to lose   ?

Not the Seven: his motivation was not enthusiasm for life

Consistently refused to be paid more than a part of the salary due to   ?
him

In his private self he had that strain of Christian faith which can   ?5
hardly wait for the life hereafter and is heedless of the physical body

Conclusion: 6-5

One of my psychic colleagues picked up a quality of self-denigration and a form
of blockage in him. Some authors have speculated on an incident of abuse in
his youth; this could explain his preference for pitching himself into thoroughly
dangerous undertakings, as a self-validating psychological compensation of
enablement that can not be denied. The free agent moreover submits to no one,
and less still from a position of command.

By itself, a daring and buccaneering attitude to life corresponds to the Seven
(7-6).

A psychological analysis of the key themes of Hitler's *Mein Kampf*

On coming to Vienna: "I was repelled by the conglomeration of races which the capital showed me" (p.113)

He observes the "de-Germanisation process" in the "Slavisation of Austria" (pp.100, 99)

Revulsion at the mixing of races; fear of the loss of racial identity =   6

The various races have a "uniform character in themselves": an "inner segregation" and a "sharp outward delimitation" (pp.258-259). Perception of sameness of appearance and, by extension, of difference = 6

His prejudice against the Jews is introduced in chapter two of the first volume

Prejudice resulting from perception of difference =   6

"The mightiest counterpart to the Aryan is represented by the Jew. In hardly any people in the world is the instinct of self-preservation developed more strongly than in the so-called 'chosen'" (p.272) "The impotence of nations, their own death from old age, arises from the abandonment of their blood purity. And this is a thing that the Jew preserves better than any other people on earth" (p.605)

Envy of strength of identity =   6

The sentiment as expressed is tinged with admiration

On the Austria of his youth: "The poison of foreign nations gnawed at the body of our nationality" (p.14)

On Marxism: "Western democracy… provides this world plague with the culture in which its germs can spread" (p.72)

Imagery of disease =   6

On the first months of the party's existence, he bemoans "the complete lack of attention we found in those days" (p.321; cf.p-442)

"We chose the red colour of our posters… in order to provoke the Left, to drive them to indignation and lead them to attend our meetings if only to break them up" (p-440)

The desire to be noticed and reacted to, whatever the outcome =   6

The members of the party must feel that hostility to them "is the pre supposition for their own right to exist" (p.319)

Spirit of antagonism =   6

He concedes that the 25-point party programme may not be ideal, but decrees that it must remain unalterable on account of its "dogmatic, creedlike formulation" (p.416)

Commitment to a position in common as an article of faith =   6

The function of propaganda is "exclusively to emphasise the one right   6
which it has set out to argue for" (p.166; cf.pp.310-311, 427-428, 577)
One-sidedness, as in a for-or-against stance = 6

Leadership of the masses should be the role of the hero (p.313)

The hero, who is looked up to for his courage as the 'man of the hour' =   6

An action is proved right by its success (p.465)   ?8

He remarks on the small size of Germany, compared to the U.K. and its Empire, the U.S., Russia, and China (p.588). Germany's "present restricted living space" needs to be increased, both for the benefit of its population, and to "free it from the danger of vanishing from the earth or of serving others as a slave nation" (p.590)

Considerations of external security =   6-7

The Third Reich was itself 8-7

The absolutism of his aims   8

In Alice Bailey's teachings, purpose is a prime attribute of the first ray
See also 'Control' in chapter ten

Hitler is 6-7 (see appendix No.6)

Quotations are taken from the 1974 edition of *Mein Kampf* published by Hutchinson & Co. (Publishers) Ltd. Used by permission of The Random House Group Ltd. and Houghton Mifflin Company

Charlie Chaplin

Cast his childhood self in a role that evokes pity and admiration, and in which many of the facts were altered accordingly

To be the object of pity, admiration =	6

Felt that by her insanity his mother had deserted him and his brother — 6

Pity recurs in his screen portrayal of the Tramp, as a victim of life — 6

To be distinguished from the emotional victim (the Two) Thousands of women with maternal instincts would write to him

As a social misfit, the Tramp does not associate with his own, but 'takes up residence' in the world of social normality — 9

His bent but unbroken spirit owes itself to the capacity for contentment of the Nine, not to the resilience of the Seven

The humour drawn from the Tramp's mishaps is of a universal and everyday kind because not partisan, topical, regional, or otherwise specialized — 9

Resistant to the introduction of speech on screen — 9

In *The Great Dictator* and *Monsieur Verdoux*, what is meant to be taken seriously is at odds with what is not — –

A clash between the competing aims of the Six and the Nine respectively: when his ideas for films became issue-based (the Six), it was as if he had a creative need to be, so to speak, in two places at once

An employee at his Swiss home, to which he moved in 1953, spoke of his "first-rate clowning" and "sixth-rate philosophy"

Authoritarian, temperamental, mean — 6

Had a preference for relationships with very young women — 5, 6, 7

This trait may be least common in the Six

His pro-Communist sympathies were nothing short of bizarre, being counter to his immense wealth and self-centredness; they were the equivalent of a bee in the bonnet — 9

Embittered by his treatment as a suspected Communist at the hands of the U.S. authorities, and by his lessening fame

Resentful = — 6

In Switzerland he vented his resentment on those around him, becoming bad-tempered, brooding, and exacting

Conclusion: 6-7 with an admixture of 9. One of my colleagues found, on psychic diagnosis, that the Six component was impaired by a relationship (the one with his mother?); that the Seven comprises a nominal percentage only, and is disorientated; and that the Nine, which by admixture comprises some 30%, is very healthy (despite item ten above).

In the view of Thomas Burke, he was "first and last an actor, possessed by this, that or other. He lives only in a role, and without it he is lost." When he would wish to withdraw into himself, instead "he is compelled to merge himself, or be merged, in an imagined and superimposed life." The imagery – though not its emptiness – is that of the Nine.

Billie Holiday

As a child, she was neglected by her mother, lacked a father-figure, and was mostly brought up by relatives and friends. Who her father was is uncertain. Her education, of which she said, "About the only thing I learnt in school was how to play hooky", ceased when she was eleven. In the same year an adult neighbour raped her. At fourteen she was a prostitute	6
On starting out in her career, singing at tables for customers' tips in Harlem nightclubs, whenever she could she would spend her time in the company of other musicians	
To belong, in 'hanging out with' =	6
To merge with, and enjoy =	9
Her vocal style is characterized by feeling; it was remarked of her that "she would sing for losers" (i.e. those who are unlucky in love).	
She confined herself to material with which she identified	6
In 1939 she was presented with the song *Strange Fruit**, first performed it, and made it her own. The audience was compelled to take notice; the room would be in darkness save for a spotlight on her, and silent	6-7
Defiance, provocation; to upset convention =	6
Lived life in the fast lane, and became a heroin addict	3, 6-7, 7
Insecure, dependent; others took advantage of her	6
See item one above	

Conclusion: 6-7

* 'Southern trees bear a strange fruit,
Blood on the leaves and blood at the root,
Black body swinging in the Southern breeze,
Strange fruit hanging from the poplar trees.
Pastoral scene of the gallant South,
The bulging eyes and the twisted mouth,
Scent of magnolia sweet and fresh,
And the sudden smell of burning flesh!
Here is a fruit for the crows to pluck,
For the rain to gather, for the wind to suck,
For the sun to rot, for a tree to drop,
Here is a strange and bitter crop.'

Strange Fruit was written by Abel Meeropol, a white Jewish schoolteacher who was a writer, poet, composer, and communist. He is 5-4.

King George VI

Nervous, shy   4-5, 6-5

According to my findings, the Five is of more effect as subtype than
his type in respect of this combination

Egalitarian, as exemplified by the duke of York camps with their   5, 7
ethos of class suppression

As president of the Industrial Welfare Society, he had a good
knowledge of factory conditions and toured shop floors

Work-related issues of wellbeing and safety =   6

Some of his speeches could not be broadcast due to the long pauses
that compensated for his stammer, which he persevered in trying
to cure. He was tormented at the prospect of having to make the
closing speech, as president of the British Empire Exhibition of
1925, and anxious that his efforts would meet with the approval
of his father, to whom he wrote, "I do hope I shall do it well, but I
shall be very frightened as you have never heard me speak." In the
event, to quote a commentator, "The speech was every bit as bad as
he imagined it would be"

Having never thought that he would be King, he was anguished
beyond words on learning that he would be. On the abdication of
Edward VIII (a very immature Seven) in 1936, he realized that he
would have to "do his best" for the institution of the monarchy, or
else "the whole fabric might crumble under the shock and strain of
tall", as he said

Commitment =   6

Prone to outbursts of rage   6, 7

The cause is likely to have been frustration

Had a dread of reviewing troops. An occasion in 1943 is recorded
when he had to be verbally coerced into doing so

Fear of being seen to stand out=   6-5

A variant of the desire of 6-5 to see without being seen: to be either
anonymous or invisible

Conclusion: 6-5

James Dean

In a school essay, he enthused over the range of interests that he felt lay open to him in life	7

Not the Three, as stimuli- and not energy-driven

Worked hard in non-academic areas at school. According to one observer, he "had to prove he was a man" (self-respect and/or gaining the respect of one's peers), and was "very hung up on being part of the crowd" (need to belong)	6

His mother, to whom he was close, had died when he was nine, whereupon he was passed to his father's sister and her husband to be raised. His father had not wished to keep him

Of his acting technique he said, "I don't know what happens when I act", and resisted its being dissected "like a rabbit in a clinical research laboratory." Nor did he have any wish to be told how to act	6 + 7

To be oneself and to conform are both traits of the Six who is aware of having to make a choice between them; in doing so, he 'takes a position'

When he can not make the choice, a conflict of impulses arises (see chapter eight)

The Four, in being himself, has no choice

It is surmised that he sought "to control the emotions and reactions of others before they controlled him"

This would make sense as a preemptive and defensive measure (the Six)

As an actor he craved attention, and resorted to shock tactics if it was not forthcoming	6-7
Rebellious	6, 7-6
Moody	4, 6
Homosexual or bisexual	5, 6, 7

Conclusion: 6-7

John Lennon

At school and art college he was bored, lazy, and confrontational towards authority	6 + 7
Made a speciality of drawings depicting deformity and the grotesque	6
See item eight below	
Humorous with a cutting edge	6
As a youngster he acted tough, respected those who stood up to him, and despised weakness	
A strength:weakness perspective =	6
His father deserted the family a few years after his birth, and his mother died in a road accident when he was seventeen	
With some school friends he formed the Quarry Men in 1957 (they became the Beatles in 1960), first playing skiffle then rock and roll	6 + 7
For the rationale of the Six and the Seven coalescing in time, see tabulation No.3 in appendix No.1	
To his young female fans he exuded an air of danger	6-7
What underlies this trait is uncertainty as to how the person will behave at close quarters, with the suspicion that he will do so aggressively	
Talented at writing nonsense passages based on wordplay and allusion	5(-4),?7
With Yoko Ono, his stunts on behalf of peace (e.g. the Amsterdam 'bed-in' of 1969) were such that they could not fail to be taken notice of	
Idealism =	5-4
Actions designed to be taken notice of =	6
Give Peace A Chance and *Imagine* have a Five content	
His compositions are a sometimes stark commentary on life as he experienced it	6

Conclusion: 6-7 with an admixture of 5

Paul McCartney is 9-1 with an admixture of 6.

Muhammad Ali

As a young lad, he was the talkative entertainer	6 + 7
Sense of racial injustice	1, 6
Single-minded in his commitment to boxing, as a black man and role model	6
His loud antics in and outside the ring had the effect of:	
Drawing attention to himself =	6-7
Disconcerting his adversary =	6

If a Six has no way of securing his position in a one-to-one situation, making the other person feel insecure can be a feasible strategy After the weigh-in with Liston in 1964, Ali said of him, "He is scared of no man, but he is scared of a nut. Now he doesn't know what I'm going to do"

In the ring he was:

Watchful for danger =	6
In constant movement, rapid and nimble =	7
As to the spectators, "I didn't care what they said long as they kept coming to see me fight"	6- 7
Converted to the Nation of Islam	
Sense of identity, belonging =	6
His conversion antagonized or left confused the black advocates of racial integration – whose side was he on?	6
In 1967 he defied the authorities by refusing to be drafted to fight in the Vietnam War, and defended his stand passionately	6

Conclusion: 6-7

Pol Pot

As an electronics student in France, he used the pseudonym 'The 6-5
Original Cambodian', and joined the French Communist Party
Connotation of ideological purity

This is the fastidiousness of the Five in an ideological setting

In April 1975 he did not enter Phnom-Penh to the cheers of the
residents – who were held to be enemies of the state – but waited a few
days until the capital was deserted as a result of their being driven out

The government was only known of to the population as Angkar: the
'Organization'

Decreed that "Those who defend us… must observe everything, but so
those being observed are unaware of it"

It was noticed that "Even in front of the camera he hides"   6-5

In a speech of July 1975 to army representatives of the party, he
declared that their coming to power had been achieved in a way that
was 'clean', being "without any foreign connection or involvement"
In his eyes the party stood in diametric contrast to all others; this
ignored the fact that it had evolvec1 under the aegis of its Vietnamese
counterpart. Likewise, when he made reference to other countries it
was in a blanket fashion, so bypassing comparison with them. His use
of the term 'clean' as above should be noted; the history of the party
was to be made 'clean', so that only homegrown revolutionary zeal
should be discerned

See item one above

Self-reliance as a commitment* =   6-5

Resorted to the imagery of disease in conveying the idea of enemies
of the state. In his mind they were too close to hand and invasive (the
Five), e.g. they were 'microbes' which "if we try to bury them", he
warned, "will rot us from within"

Imagery of disease =   6

Paranoia =   6-5

One of his various pseudonyms was Brother Number One. (Pol Pot is   3
itself a pseudonym)

Conclusion: 6-5 disintegrated to 3

*This trait has a parallel in the Juche idea of the Korean Workers' Party which
governs North Korea (6-5). The idea comprises autonomy in ideology, independence in politics, self-sufficiency in economy, and self-reliance in defence.

Dennis Nilsen

As a child, very withdrawn	5

His grandfather was the only member of the family to whom he felt a strong attachment. One day, at the age of six, he was taken to "come and see Grandad", whose body was laid out in the dining room, not having been told that he was dead

In his mind the incident fused the state of death with that of attachment

Image fixation (see chapter seven) =	5-6
As a policeman, he resigned when he could not bring himself to arrest two homosexuals, being one himself: he identified with them	6
Conducted interviews at Jobcentres	2, 5, 6, 9
Became branch secretary of the respective union, and picketed frequently	6
Could be kind and mild-mannered, or argumentative and sarcastic; dry humour	6

A dry humour is associated more with the Five

Killed some fifteen men, treating the bodies as company until he tired of them

Gave as his motive for the first murder, "I was afraid to wake him in case he left me"

Necrophilia =	5
Sense of abandonment =	6

See item two above

His behaviour towards the men whom he befriended was very in consistent. Some were strangled, others he let go unharmed. One had woken in the morning with marks of strangulation, Nilsen advising him to go to a doctor; another he resuscitated, his dog having alerted him to the fact that he was not dead	6

Conclusion: 6-5

An example of simple necrophilia is John Christie, who is 5-4.

Oliver Cromwell

As a youngster, boisterous and indulged. His sense of responsibility may have been judged to be less than optimal; the provisions of his father's will somewhat bypassed Oliver. (He was eighteen when his father died)	7

Prone to marked mood swings. It is speculated that he was hypomanic

(Hypo)mania =	7
Could be uncouth	
Lack of social sense =	4, 5
Informality =	7
Felt himself to be a crusader	1, 6
Had periodic doubts that his faith was strong enough to ensure his salvation	6

Does this account for item seven below, whereby he 'proved his faith'?

Would be carried away by excitement in battle, when it was noticed that "He did laugh so excessively as if he had been drunk; his eyes sparkled with spirits"

If as for item two above =	7

Merciless in his treatment of the Irish in 1649

The standard correlation would be with the Eight. However, it is the Six that is in evidence in what he wrote of the Irish campaign: "If ever men were engaged in a righteous cause in the world, this will scarce be second to it. We come to break the power of a company of lawless rebels, who having cast off the authority of England, live as enemies to human society"

Utilized his special status as military commander and Member of Parliament to mediate between the army, the House of Commons, and the King	7-6

Although his mediation was from the disinterested perspective of constitutionality, he would be involved in the measures decided on. This was not therefore the mediation at arm's length of a third party, as of the Five

Conclusion: 7-6. He is not what would be expected, the narrowness of his beliefs (the Six) the strangest of contrasts with what should be the liberality and unpreachiness of the Seven.

Thomas Barnardo

Having been agnostic, at the age of sixteen he became an evangelical Christian, earnest, impatient, and undaunted in saving souls	?5, ?7
Had assumed that he would be accepted by a mission to China, but he put paid to his chances by speaking out against its management	
To try to 'run before you can walk' =	7
As a medical student, he devised a scheme (not proceeded with) to speed up the course of his studies	3, 7
In bringing to notice the plight of destitute youngsters, he dramatized – if not sentimentalized – their state	2, 7
Very resourceful organizer, planner, and fund-raiser	7
After six years his activities comprised a mission church, a home for street boys and another for girls, a 'coffee palace' for working men, an employment agency for his boys, a depot for religious literature, and a magazine which he edited himself	
Many-sided activities of a reformist kind =	5+7
Systematic in teaching his boys one or another trade	5
Abducted children whom he judged to be at risk from their parents, which led to many court appearances	?
His concern with health and hygiene in the homes was remarkably enlightened, as was his attitude towards the severely handicapped	5
The lengthy agreement to which foster-parents in the U.K. had to consent was a model of ethical standards and care, and anticipated corresponding legislation by decades	5-6
This provision contrasts strangely with the readiness with which children in their thousands were sent to homes in Canada, where safeguards were more or less non-existent and some were shockingly treated	

Conclusion: 7-6 with an admixture of 5

Marlene Dietrich

Manufactured as a performer the image of a siren, which of necessity left much about her enticing yet remote, unspoken, hinted at, ambiguous: an object of fascinated attention	7
A reversal of the Seven's capacity for being fascinated (Insecurity is another reversible trait; see Muhammad Ali: the Six)	
Josef von Sternberg taught her the technicalities of meticulously crafting her screen persona; he is 5-4	
Craved validation by being wanted, which is normally a trait of the Two. She often did domestic chores for those for whom she cared at any given time	
When the image needed bolstering, she was not above artfulness	3, 7
Self-absorbed	7
Did not conform to gender stereotype in mode of dress	
To adopt a style of one's own =	4, 5-4
Defiant of convention =	6 (-7)
Not bound by convention: a 'free spirit' =	7
Bisexual	5, 6, 7
Entered into relationships on impulse	7
Accepted with bad grace that her former lovers could commit to other partners	–
This sounds like a mixture of sulkiness and selfishness, as of a child who has something enjoyable taken away from him to be shared	
See item three above	
Her attempt at an autobiography showed a complete disregard for the facts	7
"Facts are unimportant", she informed the reader	

Conclusion: 7-6, the subtype being light. Psychic diagnosis confirms that there is no subtype.

John Dillinger

As a child, lonely and sullen	6
Seemed to resent the affection that his father showed to John's stepmother and half-brother	
To feel unwanted =	2
Envious =	2, 6, 7-6
To feel excluded =	7
By the age of twelve he was the leader of a neighbourhood gang	6
Sought excitement in staying out late, thieving, and breaking into local factories or railway yards to run the machinery	7
Pranks are a pastime of the Seven who is bored	
Gained a reputation for daring	
To test boundaries ("How far do I dare to go?" or "How far can I go without being caught?") =	6
To wish to stand out by comparison ("I'm braver than you") =	6-7
Philanderer	7
Friendly and animated; could play the joker	7
Revelled in seeing himself written up in the papers	6 + 7
Agile; drove with great skill	7
Could his desire for excitement have had a constructive outlet if in his youth he had been encouraged in some form of car racing?	
His attitude towards being an outlaw in 1933/34 can be summed up as devil-may-care	7
Having escaped from gaol in March 1934, in a letter to his sister Audrey he told her not to worry as "I am having a lot of fun"	
A strange variant of the Seven's lightness of being	

Conclusion: 7-6. Psychic diagnosis confirms that there is no subtype.

Walt Disney

His journalistic cartoons were witty and light-hearted	7
A light presence of the Six, if any	
In his younger days, a practical joker	7
Could take a joke too far	?
His form of screen animation was based on childhood fun and make believe, transposed onto an animal kingdom having its own personalities	7
From the 1930s onwards he was dictatorial and over demanding towards his staff – in whom, however, he brought out the best	8
When he was displeased with an employee's efforts, the person would be told so to his face; if pleased, it would be learned of at second hand	?
The animated characters had to have ease of movement, and the widest range of expressions and body language	
Flow, range =	7
In 1933, he decided that during sketching sessions, human models would no longer be in static poses, but moving around and doing acrobatics. He started a small zoo at the studio, so that the animators could study the creatures in movement	
Was aghast at how his staff and their families misbehaved when he invited them to a free weekend of enjoyment and relaxation at a Desert Lake resort in 1938 as a reward for the success of *Snow White*	
To have a 'squeaky-clean' image =	7
Not to be confused with the Nine	
His empire would embrace publishing, merchandizing, television, Disneyland, and Disney World	7 + 8

Conclusion: 7-8

Richard Rodgers

As a small child, he experimented with chords and rhythms on the piano, and by the age of "nine or eleven" he was composing

Precocious giftedness =	7
Improvised experimentation, as in an art =	7
His nature had a lightness of being	7
Smart dresser; poised	7 (-6)

The poise may have been a form of defence

See item six below

As rehearsals for a show drew near, the effect impacted on his physical wellbeing, through an upset stomach or sleepless nights

Anxiety =	1, 6
Anticipation, in its eagerness and high hopes =	7

A physical sensation at the back of the neck told him of the audience reaction. Of one performance he wrote that the sensation "was like an actual blow"; it was a resounding success   ?7

Set store by:

Outward appearances =	3, 6
Whether a composition was approved of =	6

It was said of him that he "can be talked out of any song. He is the most frightened composer of them all. One harsh look, and he completely believes his song is no good"

Being someone who lived only through composing, his role as head of the family was half-hearted, and his dealings with the children arbitrary. His wife took charge of their income, home and family, and social engagements   7

Had he been an academic, the correlation would be with the Five or the Seven. I would suggest that his emotions were skin-deep, which is not unusual in the Seven who has a lightness of being. This does not mean that they are not real, but raises the question of how lasting (and reciprocated?) they are

By the mid-1940s he no longer felt free of cares and could be graceless, quick to take offence, and deaf to argument   6

Among the reasons was a sense of being pressurized (i.e. anxiety: "What if I fail after such successes?"). As he said, "If you lose your momentum you're dead"

Conclusion: 7-6
Oscar Hammerstein is 7-8.

Paul Robeson

At college he showed talent as an orator, debater, and singer. He was an outstanding athlete and had a magnificent physique

Diversity of talents =   7

In his oratory, he made his audience feel as he felt (the Six)

The impassioned orator could be 6-7 or 7-6. In this context it should be noted that the persuasiveness of the Three as orator is invariably mistaken for passion

Of the severe injuries that he received on the college football team he later said, speaking not as a team member but as a black person, "as their representative, I had to show that I could take whatever was handed out"

To live up to the expectations of oneself that others have, in the   6
process gaining their respect =

It is accepted that he was naive in his choice of some film roles

Naive, in being too trusting =   7

The trait was also apparent in his sympathies for communist regimes, although by itself too generalized a feature in those days to attribute to any one class of person

In the 1940s he campaigned at numerous labour union functions,   6
and urged Black participation in unions as "the best way my race can win justice,"

Hailed as a role model and spokesman for his race   6

As role model only, an alternative correlation could be with the Three

To his brother Benjamin, he had the vision of "breaking down the   6 + 7
barriers that have imprisoned his race for centuries"

In 1958 his autobiography *Here I Stand* was published

To take a position, as in the title =   6

Spoke several languages, and had some knowledge of many others   5, 7

Conclusion: 7-6

Marilyn Monroe

As a child, given to fantasizing. In one scenario she appeared naked in church for "God and everyone else to see." In another, "I dreamed of myself walking proudly in beautiful clothes and being admired by everyone and overhearing words of praise"

Fantasy as an emotional resource =	2
Desire to be the centre of attention =	2-3, 3
Need for approval =	6
Desire to be noticed =	6-7
Fantasy as a mechanism of escape from reality =	7

As she put it, "In a daydream you jump over facts as easily as a cat jumps over a fence"

Insecure; without a sense of belonging	6

At two weeks old her mother took her to neighbours who looked after her for seven years, during which time her mother would behave distantly towards her when they saw each other. Her mother then moved house, Norma Jeane rejoining her, but was committed to a mental hospital before long. The rest of her childhood was spent in a succession of foster homes and an orphanage. There was doubt as to who her father was, and when as an adult she tried to contact the man whom she understood to be her father, he did not accept her

Dramatized or fabricated episodes from her childhood

Emotional exaggeration =	2, 7
Blurring of fact and fiction =	7
Self-absorbed	7
Her state of being was precarious and ethereal. Arthur Miller compared her in some moods to "a smashed vase. It is a beautiful thing when it is intact." In a poem she compared herself to "a cobweb in the wind"	?
Unable to reach beyond the screen image that was made of her	7

Conclusion: 7-6. Psychic diagnosis confirms that the subtype is quite heavy (35%).

Frank Sinatra

As a youngster, indulged	7
This may have led to his overbearing manner	
Compulsive socializer; low boredom threshold; brash; reckless; carefree spender; smart dresser	7
Craved recognition and respect	3, 6
Was this for the sake of proving himself to his mother, for whom his success never seemed enough? If so, the correlation is with the Six	
Both generous and mean	
Oscillation over a behavioural spectrum =	6
Retaliated against adverse comment	7
See 'Retaliation' in chapter nine	
Practical joker	7
It is speculated that he was in some degree manic-depressive; if so =	7-6
His audience identified with him through the emotional images that he conjured up in song. Shirley MacLaine writes of this audience, as a feminine entity, that "He desperately needed her to love him, appreciate him, acknowledge him, and never betray his trust. So he would cajole, manipulate, caress, admonish, scold, and love her unconditionally until there was no difference between him and her"	6
Graceful, seamless vocal style	7
As was said of him, "He sings conversation like we're talking"	

Conclusion: 7-6

Nelson Mandela

In his earlier years in the ANC, confrontational	6, 7-6
In prison he sought to reach out and find common ground by discussion and education, in a climate of moderation	5 + 7
His capacity for doing this would prove decisive in the period prior to democratic elections in 1994	
By itself, moderation relates to the One or the Five	
With enormous effect he brought psychology to bear in his handling of the warders, whom in their excesses he could even regard with pity. He practiced the dictum 'Know your enemy', studying the Afrikaner mindset. He would talk with the warders in Afrikaans, and read books in the language	5
Even as a prisoner he had pride, dignity, and moral authority	–
The correlation to these traits lies elsewhere	
Of his 27 years in prison he said, "You had time to think.... to look at yourself from a distance"	5
Disarming	7 (-6)
Tenacious in his loyalties	6
Magnanimous	7
See 'Misconceptions as to type' in chapter ten	
Exceptional memory	?
Can be outspoken	5, 6
Change in South Africa has not proceeded either as smoothly or as quickly as he had hoped	3, 7

Conclusion: 7-6 integrated to 5

Oliver Tambo is 5-6. For thirty years he kept in being the external wing of the ANI by his campaigning, diplomatic skills, and travel in the outside world. The reciprocity of trust and loyalty (the Six) between Mandela in prison and Tambo in exile ma be noted.

Democratic Kampuchea, 1975–1979

The entire population became a slave labour force

Subjugation =   8

A 1975 party document asserted that "compared with the revolutions in China, Korea, and Vietnam, we are 30 years ahead of them." A party session slogan was "The Organization excels Lenin and is out-tripping Mao"

Such statements could be taken for those of a self important Three, were it not for the reckless speed with which it was intended to implement the ideology of a quasi-government – it was not even constituted until twelve months after the takeover – which was formulating measures in threadbare fashion, as if by afterthought

Reckless over-optimism =   7

The country was on the brink of starvation in April 1975; yet in September an export target of two million tons of rice was projected for 1977

As for item above =   7

A new currency was introduced on a trial basis, "because finance is the instrument of state power", then withdrawn. It was conceded that "many places have not yet used it because there's nothing to spend it on"

Naivety of outlook =   ?3, 7

Vast quantities of animal and plant products reputed to have medicinal or aphrodisiac properties were exported to China, in payment for aid

To opt for the easiest method, regardless of the (ecological) conse-   7
quences =

Chinese technicians and advisors, of whom there were 15,000,   7
complained among themselves about the irresponsible demands of the authorities, e.g. tanks and armoured cars were to be operated by boys aged 13 to 16

Delegations found that conversation with their hosts was scant, areas visited were almost deserted, and requests to talk with workers were met with evasion

This trait would seem to relate to the paranoia of Pol Pot (q.v.: 6-5)

Conclusion: 7-8. Psychic diagnosis confirms disintegration to the One.

Karl Marx

His theory of capital and labour envisaged the universal overthrow of the bourgeoisie, the abolition of private ownership, and a class-less society

Socio-economic theory =	5-6
Absolutism of concept =	8
Intellectually overbearing	5
Argumentative, outspoken	5-6, 6 (-7)
A driving force in him was anger	?8

This is not the personalized anger of the disaffected and resentful Six

Abusive wit	6

But see items two and four above

According to a Prussian spy who reported on him, his working regimen was chaotic. He could work tirelessly day and night, or achieve nothing for days on end	?

Despite the wretched circumstances in which the family lived for many years in England until becoming settled, and the ailments which constantly tormented him, his outlook was exceptionally positive

Resilience (i.e. does not give up) =	7
The strength to endure and overcome (i.e. does not go under) =	8
Anxious to keep up appearances	3, 6
Proud of his wife's aristocratic lineage	2-3, 3
In completing a questionnaire for his daughters, his answer to 'Your chief characteristic' was 'Singleness of purpose'; to 'Your idea of happiness', 'To fight'; and to 'Your idea of misery', 'Submission'	8

Conclusion: 8-7. Psychic diagnosis confirms an admixture of the Five, but not of the Six.

In his material welfare he was provided for by Engels and not self-reliant, as would be expected in an Eight.

Henry Ford

The Model T Ford was marketed to the ordinary person

Mass production =   8-9

Elements of the Nine are the continuity of the production line, and the familiarity of the operative with his tasks

Enormity of impact =   8

The car as an essential =   9

Became self-reliant by acquiring the necessary raw materials, their sites, and transportation facilities

Vertical integration =   8-9

An increase of mass (the Nine), not an extension of range (the Seven)

Hostile to trade unions and bankers

Desire to retain control =   8

In 1920 the company was reincorporated, all stock being held by members of the Ford family, and in its heyday had no borrowings

In due course he lost ground to competitors by his attachment to standardization at the cost of innovation and diversity   9

During the Great War he chartered a liner in which with other pacifists he cruised to Europe, as an exercise in 'mediation'

A tokenistic and quirky attempt to address a complex issue =   9

His newspaper, the *Dearborn Independent*, printed a series of articles which then appeared in book form as *The International Jew; the world's foremost problem*, having for its theme the supposed plan for Jewish world domination. Half a million copies of the book were bought or given away in the U.S. It was translated into sixteen languages; Hitler was conversant with the German edition. In 1927 Ford recanted; or rather, he disclaimed responsibility for the accusations made in his name. Nonetheless the book circulated in Germany and elsewhere for more than a decade thereafter

To be over-impressionable, in being seized undiscriminatingly with an idea =   9

The trait is far more common in the Nine than in 8-9

Promoted an assortment of educational, leisure, and heritage activities, in a reversion to old time and small-town values   9

Established the Ford Foundation   8

See item three above

Conclusion: 8-9, the subtype being heavy

As a trait – though not in its substance – his anti-Semitism may be compared to the pro-Communism of Charlie Chaplin (q.v.: 6-7, with reference to the admixture of the Nine).

Heinrich Himmler

Pedantic; compulsive classifier	5 (-6)
Natural disposition to having to be in the know	?

When his brother Gebhard suspected the woman to whom he was betrothed of being unfaithful and requested his help, in a letter to him Heinrich wrote, "You must curb yourself with barbaric severity"

Uncompromising code of conduct =	8

See 'Pride' in chapter ten

The architect of an Order – the SS – dedicated to "recognition of the value of the blood", the "law of blood selection"	8-9

An aspect of the Nine was the requirement to prove the existence of a pure blood line over many generations

Devised and intended to perpetuate what he presented as customs and symbols from 'the Germanic heritage'	5-4

Always found time to busy himself with obscure geo-racial notions and proposals, and to determine the rights and wrongs in cases submitted to him for racial adjudication

As for item one above =	5 (-6)
Bureaucratic mindset =	5, 9-1

Could be indecisive when action was called for that did not for sure have Hitler's sanction

By the closing years of the Second World War he was in charge of the SS, police, Gestapo, and intelligence services; the concentration camps and slave labour enterprises; the home army and armaments; racial breeding and experimentation; and 'Aryan' resettlement in Eastern Europe

Conclusion: 8-9 with an admixture of 5.

James Stewart

For him, "The most important thing about acting is to approach it as a craft"   9-8

See 'Occupations' in chapter eleven

A costar told of a film sequence which he performed again and again "until it was like a sixth sense to him, until it was like he had done it every day of his life"

Familiarity by repetition =   9

The film stereotype of him is the uncomplicated, congenial, and decent man who does not waver and wins the day in having to contend with that which is inimical to these values   9

On celebrating his seventy-fifth birthday, speaking in his home town in Indiana he said, "The things I've learned here have stayed with me all my life. This is where I made my decisions that certain things were good – hard work, community spirit, God, church, and family"

Volunteered for active service in the Second World War, flying on missions over Germany and France. He proved himself to be a responsible leader as well as a conscientious administrator   1, 6

Superstitious: on wartime missions he took a rabbit's foot with him. In every western that he made with Anthony Mann, he wore the same hat and rode the same horse; the hat would be locked in a vault so that it would not be lost or loaned out to another actor   ?

In his private life he could be absent-minded   5, 9

Conclusion: 9-1. Psychic diagnosis confirms 9-8.

Bill Haley

In the late 1940s he established a base at a radio station in Chester,   9
Pennsylvania, where he recorded, sang live, did commercials, hosted
programmes, read the news, and acted as record librarian and
part-time janitor

In this instance the relevant detail is that he practically lived at the
station, not the number of jobs that he had (the Seven)

Aimed at a fusion of country, blues, and pop styles. Bill Haley and
the Saddlemen (soon to be the Comets) were promoted as a 'cowboy
jive band'

Cross-over of styles =   7

The person who would be forever associated with the cross-over is
indeed a Seven: Elvis Presley

Described his material as 'simple' and 'down-to-earth'. Of his fans at   9
live performances he said, "I always felt I was part of it with them"

The band was expected to be clean-living, and did not have an erotic   9
image

From 1957 the releases were largely lame novelty items, remakes of   9
the original hits, and cover versions

It should be noted that a novelty in this context is not an innovation
(the Seven)

Towards the end of his life, he became severely disorientated in the   9 to 6
mind and paranoid. His conversation was nostalgic, rambling to the
point of incoherence (a worsening of the meandering tendency of the
Nine), and foul-mouthed

Conclusion: 9-8, in his last years disintegrated to 6.

His career had gone too far, too fast, and he was dragged along behind it until
for lack of sustainment it came to a halt.

Appendix 5

LIST OF COUNTRIES BY TYPE

Updated 2024

Afghanistan	Fragmented	40% of 1, 30% of 9, 20% of 6
Albania	4-5	
Argentina	3-4	
Australia	6-7	
Austria	5-6	
Bangladesh	2-1	
Belgium	5-4	
Bhutan	4-5	
Bolivia	6-7	
Brazil	8-7	very heavy (45-49%) subtype
Cambodia:		
– as Democratic Kampuchea		
– 1975-1979	7-8	disintegrated to 1
– present day	5-6	
Canada	5-6	
China	8-8	no subtype
Cuba	7-6	
Denmark	7-6	
Ecuador	4-3	
Egypt	6-7	
England – approx. 1220-1715	3-4	
(from 1707: United Kingdom)	Queen Elizabeth 1: 7-8	
Estonia	4-5	
Finland	5-4	
France – approx. 1455-1790	7-8	
France – from approx. 1790	5-6	
Germany – until approx. 1935	6-7	
Germany – from approx. 1935	8-7	
Greece	7-7	no subtype
Iceland	4-5	

India	9-1	
Indonesia	7-8	
Iran	1-9	
Iraq	6-7	
Ireland	9-8	
Israel	4-5	very heavy (45-49%) subtype
Italy	3-4	
Jamaica	3-3	no subtype
Japan – until 1945	6-7	
Japan – from 1945	5-5	no subtype
Jordan	7-6	
Korea – North	6-5	disintegrated to 3
Korea – South	7-6	
Kuwait	3-2	
Lebanon	Fragmented	40% of 4
Luxembourg	4-5	
Malaysia	6-7	
Mexico	7-7	no subtype
Myanmar	9-1	disintegrated to 6
Nepal	5-6	
New Zealand	7-7	no subtype
Nigeria	3-2	
Norway	5-5	no subtype
Pakistan	6-7	
Peru	6-7	
Philippines	2-3	
Portugal – approx. 1475-1720	3-3	
Portugal – from approx. 1720	9-8	
Qatar	5-4	
Russia	6-7	
Rwanda	6-5	
Saudi Arabia	1-9	
Singapore	1-2	
South Africa	8-9	
former Soviet Union	6-7	

Spain – until approx. 1770	5-4	
Spain – from approx. 1770	6-7	
Sri Lanka	6-7	
Sweden	5-6	
Switzerland	5-4	integrated to 8
Syria	6-5	
Taiwan	3-3	no subtype
Thailand	6-7	
Turkey	6-7	
United Arab Emirates	3-4	
United Kingdom	9-1	
U.S.A. – until approx. 1865	6-7	
U.S.A. – from approx. 1865	3-2	
Vietnam* – present day	6-7	
Yemen	4-5	disintegrated to 2

* The now superseded Democratic Republic of Vietnam, established in 1945, is also 6-7. The Republic of Vietnam ('South Vietnam'), which was absorbed into the unitary state in 1976, is fragmented, having about 30% of 3 and 40% of 6.

Appendix 6

LIST OF PERSONALITIES OF THE THIRD REICH BY TYPE

Martin Bormann	8-9	
Adolf Eichmann	5-6	
Joseph Goebbels	3-	no subtype
Hermann Goring	3-4	
Rudolf Hess	5-4	
Reinhard Heydrich	7-	no subtype
Heinrich Himmler	8-9	
Adolf Hitler	6-7	disintegrated to 3
William Joyce ('Lord Haw-Haw')	5-6	
Josef Mengele	6-5	
Joachim von Ribbentrop	3-2	
Leni Riefenstahl	7-	no subtype
Ernst Rohm	7-6	
Erwin Rommel	7-6	
Alfred Rosenberg	–	no type
Albert Speer	5-6	
Julius Streicher	3-2	

According to psychic diagnosis, Hitler began disintegrating to the Three in the autumn of 1926. His executive authority over the NSDAP had been consolidated at a meeting of the party in May of that year.

To watch Eichmann defending himself in court with his protestations of obedience and loyalty (he sheltered behind legalisms: "Legally, I had no choice but to carry out the orders I received"), one could be excused for supposing him to be a Six – albeit his protestations were pedantic and testy, almost prim (the Five). He was a nobody until his career began in 1934 as a government records clerk organizing a card index of German Jews, and was persistent in improving on ways and means first for the dispersal, then the elimination, of European Jewry. This was not the enthusiasm of the Seven, but the zeal of unquestioning commitment (the Six) in a technocrat (the Five), with the Six subtext of affirmation by approval. A colleague of his, Wilhelm Höttl, has stated that Eichmann was "desperate to show that he was capable." Or as he himself would later say, "I resolved to show how well a job could be done." In 1950 he fled to Argentina where he had a lack of job success, his motivation to achieve having fallen away.

Mengele could be expected to be 5-6 and not 6-5 (see 'Cast of mind' in chapter seven); he was however fanatical (the Six). The Five subtype is very heavy (45%).

www.ingramcontent.com/pod-product-compliance
Lightning Source LLC
La Vergne TN
LVHW051727080426
835511LV00018B/2926